CONTENTS

THE LAWWAY WITH LAWYERS

THE SHIFTING SANDS OF LAW

Forward by:-
Hon'ble Chancellor Shri Ajay Prakash Shrivastava
Maharishi University of Information Technology

Editors:-
Mr. Arun Kumar
Dr. Ritu Singh Meena

The Shifting Sands of Law

Edited by: - Mr. Arun kumar

              Dr. Ritu Singh Meena

ISBN: - 978-93-100-0244-7

Printed in: - India

Published by: - the lawway with lawyers

A/49 sector2 Dhurwa Ranchi 834004

thelawwaywithlawyers@gmail.com

https://www.thelawwaywithlawyers.com/

About the Book

The editors published this edited book to meet the needs of all participants in the legal academic community as well as Indian citizens because law is a dynamic concept that evolves to meet societal needs. In order for the general public to understand what is going on in the legal world and what sorts of rights and remedies they have, this book contains a great deal of current concerns that have been written about by numerous scholars and law students. For individuals who are serious about learning the law, this book is a fantastic resource. Teachers, students beginning their first law course, and anybody else interested in law and legal procedure should read this book.

FOREWORD

Hon'ble Chancellor Shri Ajay Prakash Shrivastava
Maharishi University of Information Technology

This book is the collection of various legal aspects and the editors did the excellent work to put this ideas into this edited book. The books have contemporary issues and their solution in the most simple language. And when I read this book I saw that today's generation is more concern and aware about their rights and they want to spread the knowledge into the society.

The books lays emphasis on the laws and their practical application and it is great approach by the editors and law students to put the diverse issue into this single book.

The editors come up with this excellent and well-written book and attempt have been made to make every chapter of this book up-to-date by giving the leading judgments of the various courts. I hope this book will prove very useful for the law students, teachers and also for the courts.

Jai Guru Dev !

Shri Ajay Prakash Shrivastava
Noida, Uttar Pardesh
20 September 2023

<u>ABOUT THE EDITORS</u>

Mr. Arun Kumar is Assistant Professor of Law at Maharishi Law School at Maharishi University of Information Technology, Noida. Mr. Kumar has authored a books Dowry Deaths: The Burning Issue (2022) and "Law and Research Methodology (2023). In addition to this he has published more than 30 Research Papers, Articles, book chapters in edited volumes and UGC care, Peer reviewed journals; presented papers in several National and International Seminars/Conferences. He is Active Reviewer of many International Journals and also a member of Editorial Board in reputed Journals. He has obtained the degree of B.A LL.B and LL.M (Criminal Law) from CCS University Meerut and Maharishi University of Information Technology, Noida respectively. Mr. Kumar has substantial experience of Criminal Law and Family Law. His area of interest includes Human Rights, Child Rights.

Dr. Ritu Singh Meena is Assistant Professor of Political Science at Maharishi Law School at Maharishi University of Information Technology, Noida. Dr. Ritu has Three books to her credit- Women Empowerment in Bangladesh: Policies and Achievements, Dowry Deaths: The Burning Issue(2022) and "Law and Research Methodology (2023).In addition to this she has published approximately 30 Research Papers, book chapters in edited volumes, Peer reviewed journals; presented papers in several National and International Seminars/Conferences. She is a member of Editorial Board in reputed Journals. She has been awarded Ph.D.in International Studies from JamiaMilliaIslamia New Delhi. She has been sponsored by ICSSRunder the Data Collection Abroad scheme for her Ph.D. research work data collection in Bangladesh in 2018. She has also awarded with Rajiv Gandhi National Fellowship for Research Work.Her research interests are International Issues, Gender Sensitivity etc.

ACKNOWLEDGMENT

The editors spent many hours conducting research for this book. Every piece of the author's work that was used in this book has been fully acknowledged. This book is the best resource for comprehending the fundamental ideas of the law, which are essential for someone who wants to learn about the law.

To begin with, we are thankful to the Hon'ble Prof. Ajay Prakash Shrivastava (Chancellor, Hon'ble Prof. (Dr.) Bhanu Pratap Singh, Vice Chancellor and Prof. (Group Captain) O.P. Sharma, Director General of Maharishi University of Information Technology, Ajay kumar Yadav, Ajmi soja, Shahid istyak and all the lawway with lawyers team for helping us by providing the full support and knowledge.

ANALYZING THE RUSSIA-UKRAINE CONFLICT IN LIGHT OF WAR CRIMES

Authored by:- Mr. Radha Ranjan

ABSTRACT

A complicated and lengthy international crisis has developed out of the Russia-Ukraine war, which started in 2014 with Russia's annexation of Crimea and subsequent participation in Eastern Ukraine. By examining the conflict through the prism of war crimes, this study aims to provide light on the alleged transgressions of international humanitarian law committed by both Russian and Ukrainian forces as well as non-state entities engaged in the fight. This analysis, which draws from a variety of primary and secondary sources, aims to give a thorough overview of the war crimes that were allegedly committed during the conflict, including but not limited to indiscriminate shelling, targeting of civilian populations, the use of prohibited weapons, and allegations of torture and illegal detention.

This study also looks at how the international community and international organisations have responded to accusations of war crimes during the Russia-Ukraine conflict. of a setting marked by ongoing battles, information warfare, and geopolitical complexity, it examines the difficulties of identifying and prosecuting war crimes. The research also examines how these alleged war crimes may affect the likelihood of regional conflict resolution and peace-making. This study intends to contribute to a fuller understanding of the humanitarian dimensions of the conflict and its impact on international law, diplomacy, and the pursuit of justice through a critical examination of the Russia-Ukraine conflict in light of war crimes. It emphasises how crucial it is to deal with war crimes in order to end the crisis sustainably, preserve the rules of international law, and ensure that individuals in the area who have violated human rights and international humanitarian law are held accountable.

Keywords: Russia, Ukraine, War, Crimes, International, Humanitarian

INTRODUCTION

Eastern Europe has been gripped by a protracted crisis with several facets since the Russia-Ukraine conflict broke out in 2014. Beyond its geopolitical implications, the battle has shone a gloomy focus on purported war crimes committed by various parties involved. A thorough examination of the Russia-Ukraine conflict in the context of war crimes is undertaken in this essay in an effort to sort through the intricate web of transgressions of international humanitarian law and their far-reaching effects.

Russia's annexation of Crimea and subsequent assistance for separatist movements in Eastern Ukraine are the two events that first sparked the conflict. War crimes accusations multiplied as the fighting escalated. These accusations cover a wide range of transgressions, including the indiscriminate shelling of residential areas, the targeting of non-combatants, the employment of weapons that are not allowed, and charges of torture and illegal detention. These atrocious atrocities are allegedly the work of non-state entities, as well as Russian and Ukrainian soldiers. This examination looks at how the international society and the global community have responded to these alleged war crimes as well, in addition to cataloguing them. In the midst of ongoing battles and disinformation campaigns, documenting and prosecuting war crimes poses enormous difficulties. However, addressing war crimes is essential for furthering chances for peace and conflict settlement in the region as well as for ensuring that justice is served. In order to find a lasting solution to this ongoing crisis, this study aims to present a thorough analysis of the Russia-Ukraine conflict through the prism of war crimes, emphasising the humanitarian ramifications of these crimes and the need for responsibility. Armed conflicts around the world, both international and non-international, have been a common occurrence since before the world wars. Including and following the world wars, armed conflicts have significantly increased both in terms of the number and intensity of such conflicts. War is a type of armed conflict between states through their military, governments, and so on, characterized by extreme violence, death, destruction, etc. Since many years now, wars are governed by laws and rules laid down by instruments of International Humanitarian Law, such as the Hague Convention, and the Geneva Conventions with its Additional Protocols. Now, war crimes are also defined under Article 8 of the Rome Statute of the International Criminal Court.

According to these laws and rules, particularly the Rome Statute, such types of crimes can broadly be categorized as follows.

These rules aim to protect people who are non-combatants, civilians, medical officials, prisoners of wars, the sick and wounded, etc. The very recent example of a major armed conflict or war is the Russia-Ukraine conflict. Although the current conflict began when Russia invaded Ukraine on 24th February 2022, however, the conflict is continuing from Russia's annexation of Crimea in 2014. This conflict has witnessed severe atrocities, loss of life, and crimes against peace and humanity.

In light of this, it becomes crucial to examine whether these atrocities fit into the definition of war crime as understood from international instruments and judicial precedents so that some action may be taken against the offenders. Further, it also becomes important to determine whether President Vladimir Putin can also be considered a war criminal and whether or how can he be made to punish for his actions against humanity and peace.

JUDICIAL PRONOUNCEMENTS

Judicial pronouncements are the formal judgements, decisions, or rulings that are made by courts of law. To resolve legal issues, these decisions interpret and apply the law, establishing legal precedents that direct subsequent cases. They are crucial in determining the legal system's structure and preserving the rule of law.

In the past, there have been several trials to punish war criminals such as the renowned *Nuremberg* and *Tokyo* trials. In this section, we will look at some of these judgments to understand how what are the essentials of war crimes and how war criminals can be punished. In the case of Prosecutor v. Germain Katanga This case involved 4 charges of war crimes for attacking the Bogoro village in the Democratic Republic of Congo (DRC) with the Ngiti militia. DRC has ratified the Rome Statute. The Chamber held that it was proven beyond any reasonable doubt that Germain Katanga had contributed significantly to the commission of crimes by the militia and was acting with common purpose. The common plan was inclusive of *"the crimes of murder, attacking civilians, destroying property, and pillaging"*. Furthermore, he was the intermediary between the weapons and suppliers and the militia committing the crimes. In addition, he used his position to use an aircraft for transporting weapons. All of this was considered to be a violation of the provisions of the Rome Statute, along with the Geneva Convention.

In the case of Prosecutor v. Thomas Lubanga Thomas Lubanga was the Founder and President of an organized armed group and was held to be responsible for several war crimes but most importantly for recruiting children under the age of 15 years voluntarily or forcefully. These children were forced to undergo harsh training and were also given severe punishments. The were forced to take active part in fighting and were also used as military guards. Lubanga was involved in all operations regarding recruitment, military operations, etc.

In the case of the Prosecutor v. Bosco Ntaganda Mt. Ntaganda was held to be guilty of almost 18 counts of war crimes and crimes against humanity. These crimes included murder, rape, deportation, intentional attacking of civilians, inducting and using children under 15 years of age in an armed conflict, sexual slavery, persecution, and so on. He was found guilty is a direct perpetrator for three crimes, murder under war crimes and crimes against humanity, along with persecution under crimes against humanity. For the rest of the crimes, he was held liable as an indirect perpetrator.

COMPARATIVE STUDY: OTHER INSTANCES OF PROSECUTING LEADERS FOR WAR CRIMES AND CRIMES AGAINST HUMANITY

We see that in the past, several leaders have been prosecuted for war crimes in nations like Bosnia, Rwanda, and Cambodia. This trend can be witnessed from one of the oldest war crimes cases like Nuremberg and Tokyo trial to recent cases before ad hoc tribunals.

Some noteworthy examples which could be relevant to the Russia-Ukraine conflict are:

SR. NO.	NAME OF THE LEADER	NATIONALITY
1	Charles Taylor	Former President of Liberia
2	Hashim Thaci	Former President of Kosovo
3	Omar al-Bashir	Former President of Sudan
4	Slobodan Milošević	Former President of Yugoslavia

In the case of the Liberian case: Charles Taylor This case was before a Special Court for Sierra Leone established by UN and Sierra Leone's government. Taylor, the former President of Liberia led a rebel group and assisted the commission of several crimes. The laws relied upon included the Statute of the Special Court for Sierra Leone, the ICCPR, Geneva Conventions, Convention against Torture, and so on. He was sentenced to 50 years of imprisonment, also upheld by the appeal. He was the first Head of State who was convicted by an internal tribunal following World War II.

In the case the case of Kosovo: Hashim thaci The Specialist Chamber in The Hague, established to deal with cases of crimes by the Kosovo Liberation Army, indicted President Thaci for war crimes and crimes against humanity, including for murder, persecution, torture, forced disappearances and so on in June 2020. Due to this he also resigned from his post and entered a detention facility in The Hague along with others.

In the case of the Sudanese Situation: Omar al-Bashir Bashir is suspected of several crimes against humanity under Article 7 of the Rome Statute, war crimes under Article 8 of the Rome Statute, and genocide under Article 6 of the Rome Statute in Darfur, Sudan. He is not the custody of ICC. Warrants have been issued but ICC has cited extreme non-cooperation and has referred the case to the UN Security Council and Assembly of the States Parties to take necessary measures.

CRITICAL ANALYSIS

Let's start with a critique of the paper's introduction, which discusses how war crimes might be used to analyse the Russia-Ukraine conflict:

Clarity and Focus: The introduction clearly focuses on the Russia-Ukraine conflict and how it relates to alleged war crimes. The reader can get their bearings because it succinctly describes the conflict's essential components, such as the annexation of Crimea and support for separatist movements.

significance of War Crimes: By emphasising the seriousness of purported violations of international humanitarian law, the introduction successfully shows the significance of war crimes in the context of the conflict. For grasping the importance of the analysis, this connection is crucial.

Comprehensive Overview: It claims to give a thorough analysis of the conflict and the war crimes that have been committed as a result, indicating a thorough investigation of the subject. However, it would be advantageous to quickly outline the analysis's focus (such as particular instances, statutory frameworks, or historical backdrop) to let the reader understand what to expect.

Engagement and intrigue: Although it effectively introduces the topic, it could be more captivating. Including a provocative question, an eye-opening fact, or an engaging narrative may help to better engage readers.

Balance and Neutrality: The introduction keeps a neutral and balanced tone, which is essential when talking about a complicated and politically touchy subject like the conflict between Russia and Ukraine. This strategy improves the credibility of the paper.

Structure and duration: It follows a succinct structure and duration that is appropriate for an introduction. Without drowning the reader in information, it delivers a suitable summary.

In sum, by clearly outlining the topic, relevance, and scope of the analysis, the introduction establishes a strong basis for the work. It prepares the ground for a thorough investigation of the conflict between Russia and Ukraine in light of war crimes. A little bit more precise information on the topics the study will cover, however, can improve it and make it more interesting.

CONCLUSION AND SUGGESTIONS

Russia and Ukraine have both refused to ratify the Rome Statute, which established the ICC. Russia revoked its signature from a statute that it had signed but not ratified in November 2016. The statute has yet to be ratified by Ukraine. Ukraine, on the other hand, has said twice that it recognizes the Court's power to conduct criminal investigations on Ukrainian territory, as specified in Article 12.3 of the Statute. Regardless of nationality, the ICC can investigate and prosecute anybody accused of committing crimes within the Court's jurisdiction on Ukrainian territory. Vladimir Putin and other significant Russian officials are examples. The probe also looks into possible criminal behavior by Ukrainian lawmakers and military personnel. The ICC only opens investigations when governments are unable or unwilling to pursue the crimes themselves, according to the principle of complementarity.

The following are the primary issues identified in this context:

The ICC's probe has political ramifications since it underscores the necessity for justice for war crimes and crimes against humanity of the magnitude of those allegedly committed in Ukraine. Despite its limited success to yet, the ICC has the potential to grow thanks to unparalleled backing. In the best-case scenario, publishing the findings of the investigations would discourage Russian military officers from bombing civilian targets and committing other war crimes, or it could hurt the regime. Furthermore, numerous experts are afraid that the proceedings may limit President Putin's options for escape.

To address such impunity, I propose using universal jurisdiction as an additional powerful tool. Its main point is that other countries can investigate crimes committed in other countries, regardless of where they occurred or the nationality or residence of the victims or potential perpetrators. Given that such acts endanger global security. There is also a more limited approach to universal jurisdiction. If a citizen of another country is accused of committing an international crime, the crime was perpetrated against a resident of this country, or the suspect resides in that country, criminal prosecution begins in that country. It lessens the pressure on the Ukrainian court system and makes criminal punishment easier. To pursue those guilty of the most egregious atrocities, about 150 countries have adopted the Geneva Conventions and other international criminal and humanitarian law standards.

1 Doctoral Research Scholar, Department of law and Governance, Central University of South

Bihar, India, NAAC Accredited A++ Grade University, Email ID – murarieflu@gmail.com,

Art. 8, Rome Statute.

3 The Prosecutor v. Germain Katanga, ICC-01/04-01/017.

4 The Prosecutor v. Thomas Lubanga, ICC-01/04-01/06.

5 The Prosecutor v. Bosco Ntaganda, ICC-01/04-02/06.

6 The Prosecutor v. Charles Ghankay Taylor, SCSL-03-01-A.

7 Specialist Prosecutor v. Hashim Thaçi, Kadri Veseli, Rexhep Selimi and Jakup Krasniqi, Case No. KSC-BC- 2020-06.

8 The Prosecutor v. Omar Hassan Ahmad Al Bashir, ICC-02/05-01/09.

9 Article 7, Rome Statute.

10 Article 8, Rome Statute.

11 Article 6, Rome Statute.

BIBLIOGRAPHY

1. Art. 8, Rome Statute.

2. The Prosecutor v. Germain Katanga, ICC-01/04-01/017.

3. The Prosecutor v. Thomas Lubanga, ICC-01/04-01/06.

4. The Prosecutor v. Bosco Ntaganda, ICC-01/04-02/06.

5. https://www.theguardian.com/world/2022/mar/17/vladimir-putin-war-criminal-Ukraine-Russia-president-justice.

6. The Prosecutor v. Charles Ghankay Taylor, SCSL-03-01-A.

7. Specialist Prosecutor v. Hashim Thaçi, Kadri Veseli, Rexhep Selimi and Jakup Krasniqi, Case No. KSC-BC-2020-06.

8. The Prosecutor v. Omar Hassan Ahmad Al Bashir, ICC-02/05-01/09.

9. Article 7, Rome Statute.

10. Article 8, Rome Statute.

11. Article 6, Rome Statute.

12. Sloboden Milošević, Kosovo, Croatia & Bosnia, IT-02-54.

13. https://www.ohchr.org/en/press-releases/2022/10/un-commission-has-found-array- war-crimes-violations-human-rights-and.

14. https://www.europarl.europa.eu/RegData/etudes/BRIE/2022/733525/EPRS_BRI(2022)73 3525_EN.pdf.

15. https://www.ohchr.org/sites/default/files/documents/countries/ua/2022-09- 23/ReportUkraine-1Feb-31Jul2022-en.pdf.

16. https://www.icj-cij.org/public/files/case-related/182/182-20221019-WRI-01-00-EN.pdf.

<u>EUTHANASIA AN INDIAN PERSPECTIVE</u>

Authored By :- AMOL YADAV

ABSTRACT

This research paper delves into the intricate and evolving landscape of euthanasia within the Indian context. With a focus on legal, ethical, and societal dimensions, the paper provides a comprehensive analysis of the perspectives surrounding euthanasia in India.

The society in which we survive in, the palliative care and quality of life issues in patients with terminally illnesses like cancer etc. have come out as an important concern for the clinicians. Parallel to this concern has been another controversial issue rolling down as named "Euthanasia" of terminally ill patients. Euthanasia as a practice allows an individual with right to autonomy that entitles the people to choose the way of their own painless death. With this as a view the opponents feel that a physician's role in the death of an individual violates the central tenet and belief of the medical profession.

Although as to be considered illegal in several countries, euthanasia has several advocates in the form of voluntary organizations like, "death with dignity", "to free someone from the immense pain" etc. In India the concept of euthanasia has been a blown practice as not being allowed in the clinical practices but has got a fillip in the reality as after the judgement of the Supreme Court in the Aruna Shaunbag Case . Coming out as a legal practice in India, only passive euthanasia gets the drift as the concept of active euthanasia still remains restricted and illegal to be practiced. What more remains is to see how long the debates go before this sensitive issue rattles the Indian legislature.

Keywords: Euthanasia, Indian context, Legal dimensions, Ethical perspectives, Terminally ill patients, Supreme Court judgment

1.   INTRODUCTION

The remarkable progress achieved in the field of medical science and technology has not been devoid of significant societal impacts. These advancements have brought to light issues that are reshaping human lifestyles and societal principles. Concurrently, there has been a surge in the recognition of human rights, individual autonomy, and the freedom to make choices. These matters necessitate a reassessment of our existing notions of societal norms, medical ethics, and value systems.

Amidst these developments, the matters of palliative care and the quality of life for individuals afflicted with terminal illnesses such as advanced cancer and acquired immune deficiency syndrome (AIDS) have emerged as crucial domains of clinical concern and research. Notable strides have been taken to extend the research agenda on palliative care and quality of life to encompass the clinical challenges faced by cancer patients. This includes efforts that delve into mental health aspects, including neuropsychiatric conditions and psychological symptoms among those with terminal medical conditions. Nonetheless, the most pertinent and clinically significant mental health issues within palliative care pertain to the wish for death and the concept of physician-assisted suicide (PAS), particularly in relation to depression. The concept of the wish for death has been posited as a fundamental construct underpinning various related phenomena, including suicidal tendencies, interest in PAS/euthanasia, and requests for PAS/euthanasia. Initially introduced by Brown and colleagues and further elaborated by Chochinov et al., this construct delves into the extent to which an individual desires an expedited end to their life. It spans from immediate suicidal intent to a complete absence of any desire for death.

Calls advocating for patient autonomy in determining the manner and timing of their own death have grown increasingly prominent in recent years. This movement has been sparked by high-profile cases involving individuals like Drs. Jack Kevorkian, Timothy Quill, and Aruna Shanbaug, which have spotlighted the challenges faced by terminally ill patients nearing the end of life. However, amidst the political and legal debates, what often goes unnoticed is the significance of medical, social, and psychological factors (such as depression) that may contribute to thoughts of suicide, the desire for hastened death, or requests for PAS among those with terminal illnesses.

2.   UNDERSTANDING THE MEANING OF EUTHANASIA AND PHYSICIAN-ASSISTED SUICIDE (PAS)

The phrase "euthanasia" was coined by English philosopher Sir Francis Bacon in the early 17th century. The term is derived from the Greek words "eu" meaning "good," and "thanatos," meaning "death," originally signifying a painless or "good" death. Euthanasia is defined as the administration of a lethal substance by one person to another, usually a patient, to alleviate unbearable and incurable suffering. This act is typically motivated by mercy to end the patient's pain. Euthanasia is carried out by physicians and categorized as either "active" or "passive." Active euthanasia involves a physician intentionally taking actions to terminate a patient's life, while passive euthanasia involves withholding or discontinuing life-sustaining treatment.

There are three forms of active euthanasia. Voluntary euthanasia occurs at the patient's explicit request. Involuntary euthanasia, also known as "mercy killing," involves ending a patient's life without their request to relieve suffering. Non-voluntary euthanasia takes place when a patient cannot give consent.

In contrast, Physician-Assisted Suicide (PAS) involves a physician providing a patient with medication or guidance to end their own life. Although theoretical and ethical distinctions between euthanasia and PAS may be subtle, the practical differences are noteworthy. Terminally ill patients might have access to potentially lethal drugs, sometimes prescribed by their physicians, without actually using them to end their lives.

Legally and ethically, both euthanasia and PAS are differentiated from the administration of high-dose pain medication that might hasten death (known as the "rule of double effect") or the withdrawal of life support. The crux of this distinction lies in the intent behind the action. In euthanasia/PAS, the goal is to end the patient's life, whereas with pain medication administration, the objective is to alleviate suffering.

Comparatively, the contrast between withdrawing life support and euthanasia/PAS is clearer. Historical legal cases have upheld a patient's right to refuse unwanted treatment, even if it results in death. However, patients have not traditionally had the right to demand specific interventions. Consequently, a patient reliant on life support can choose to end their life, while one not dependent on such support lacks this right.

3.   GLOBAL EUTHANASIA

The domain of international humanitarian law does not establish a "right to die." The notion of a "right to a good death" cannot be derived from the conventional interpretation of any human rights document. Instead, human rights documents emphasize the duty of states to safeguard and preserve the lives of all individuals. Out of the 193 member states of the United Nations (UN), merely four have legalized euthanasia: the Netherlands, Belgium, Luxembourg, and Canada. This topic remains a subject of intense debate, with many legislative bodies rejecting it. The Convention on the Rights of Persons with Disabilities, enacted in 2006, is a UN international human rights treaty aimed at safeguarding the rights and dignity of individuals. The treaty asserts that individuals with disabilities must have the same right as others to the effective enjoyment of the right to life. The International Covenant on Civil and Political Rights (ICCPR) of 1966 and the Convention on the Rights of the Child (CRC) also emphasize the inherent right to life for all individuals. Furthermore, ICCPR's Article 7 underscores the need to protect individuals from inhumane or degrading treatment.

Euthanasia was legalized in the Netherlands in 2001 through the Termination of Life on Request and Assisted Suicide (Review of Procedures) Act. This law permits euthanasia and doctor-assisted suicide under specific conditions, including the patient's wishes and medical supervision. Similarly, Belgium's Act on euthanasia, enacted in 2002, allows doctors to assist terminally ill patients who express a desire to hasten their death. Stringent legal conditions and procedures govern the application of euthanasia in Belgium.

Luxembourg decriminalized euthanasia in 2009, allowing terminally ill individuals to end their lives with the approval of two doctors and a panel of specialists. In Canada, voluntary active euthanasia, termed "physician-assisted dying," is legal for individuals over 18 with a terminal illness. This change came about due to a Supreme Court ruling in Cartar v. Canada (Attorney General). In contrast, euthanasia remains illegal in China and Hong Kong due to cultural and legal reasons.

The legality of euthanasia varies across nations. While active euthanasia is permitted in Germany, passive euthanasia hinges on the patient's written wish to stop life-prolonging measures. In the United States, active euthanasia is generally illegal, but physician-assisted suicide is legalized in certain states. A distinction exists between euthanasia and physician-assisted suicide, with the latter being permitted in states like Oregon, Washington, and Montana. In the US, life support can be withdrawn upon a patient's request. The doctor evaluates the patient's desire to end their life when deciding on life support withdrawal.

4.   EUTHANASIA AND PAS IN CLINICAL PRACTICE

Various surveys document euthanasia and Physician-Assisted Suicide (PAS) occurrence among healthcare professionals. For example, a 1995 anonymous survey of Washington physicians found that 26% received PAS requests, with two-thirds granting them. This suggests PAS is not rare, although legality concerns might prevent acknowledgment. San Francisco physicians attending AIDS patients had more striking outcomes. 98% received PAS requests, with over half granting them. In response to a hypothetical scenario, nearly half would grant an initial PAS request. A notable study surveyed critical care nurses, where 17% received PAS requests, 11% granted them, and 5% hastened death without consent (non-voluntary euthanasia). 4.7% expedited death without physician knowledge. These acts aimed to ease patient suffering, influenced by nursing's palliative role, though methodology biases were noted.

In contrast, The Netherlands, where PAS and euthanasia have been practiced for over two decades, provides data on the frequency of assistance in dying and the proportion of terminally ill patients whose lives end this way. Legalized in 1984, euthanasia in The Netherlands requires specific conditions, including explicit patient requests, agreement between patient and physician on unbearable suffering, consultation with a second physician, and proper documentation. Studies have shown that euthanasia and PAS accounted for about 4.7% of deaths in The Netherlands in 1995, a significant increase from a 1991 study reporting 2.7% involvement of medical assistance.

While supporters of PAS cite Dutch data to demonstrate responsible use, critics argue that the rise from 2.7% to 4.7% implies an increase in frequency and potentially inappropriate cases. A 1994 Dutch Supreme Court decision extended euthanasia/PAS to non-terminal chronic illnesses, sparking concerns of a "slippery slope" where eligibility expands beyond suitable candidates, like physically healthy but clinically depressed individuals.

5.   EUTHANASIA IN CLINICAL PRACTICE IN INDIA

Under Indian legal regime the Indian Penal Code, 1860 be the verdict that deals with the provisions of Active and Passive euthanasia, it as well defines to us about PAS. Active euthanasia is in the bubble of Section 302 (Punishment for Murder) of IPC and is regarded as a crime of Murder or at least a crime under Section 304 which denotes the punishment for culpable homicide not amounting to murder.

As there are two heads being used while explaining euthanasia these two are distinctive from each other at a slide, euthanasia and physician-assisted death are separated from each other as a provision over the question that 'who administers the lethal dose'. While in euthanasia, a doctor, legal practitioner or any third party does so, in PAS, the patient himself carries out the procedure.

Under Indian legal system PAS stands as illegal and a crime under Section 306 IPC defining Abetment to Suicide. Be it euthanasia or PAS, the patient has to troll through the Indian courts as courts in India have never administered a clear ruling over the issue. There have always been a tussle between people who support and oppose the provision of euthanasia. People claims that the hospitals do not listen to what the patients requests for especially in cases where the patients are terminally ill or are unable to respond to medical treatment. The psychiatrists must deal with mental capacity difficulties of the patients on regular basis. There is an urgent need for empirical research to be conducted in India to know the perceptions and attitudes of the society towards euthanasia as there has been ample of professionals and even the general public developing meaningful conclusions on whether or not euthanasia should be legalised as a clinical practice.

The legal status of passive euthanasia though varies across the nations but in India it has a positive view. As in India there is no hard and fast rule or any law specifically about euthanasia, but the mechanism works around the Supreme Court's guidelines as they are the said law until the parliament steps in to take over the role.

6.   THE INDIAN REALITY

In a nation marked by unaddressed human rights concerns, widespread illiteracy, inadequate access to clean water, prevalent infections leading to daily fatalities, and a lack of comprehensive medical assistance, discussions around euthanasia and Physician-Assisted Suicide (PAS) might be perceived as secondary. However, India's socio-religious, educational, and cultural diversities necessitate a nuanced examination of the euthanasia debate, complicated further by the presence of laws penalizing suicide attempts. The Medical Council of India, during its ethics committee meeting in February 2008, provided insights on euthanasia. It deemed practicing euthanasia unethical but recognized the potential consideration of withdrawing life-sustaining measures after brain death. The decision to withdraw support systems was proposed to be made by a designated team of doctors, including the patient's attending physician, the Chief Medical Officer or designated hospital officer, and a doctor nominated as per the Transplantation of Human Organs Act, 1994.

In India, euthanasia is classified as a criminal act. Sections 309 and 306 of the Indian Penal Code address attempted suicide and abetment of suicide, respectively, both carrying legal consequences. Only individuals declared brain dead can have life support withdrawn, with family involvement. The Supreme Court has interpreted Article 21 of the Constitution, safeguarding the right to life, as not encompassing the right to die. The Court has emphasized Article 21's role in protecting life and personal liberty, with no inference for the termination of life. However, pro-euthanasia organizations, notably the Death with Dignity Foundation, advocate for the legalization of individuals' right to choose their own demise.

A significant legal milestone occurred on March 7, 2011, when the Supreme Court permitted passive euthanasia. While refusing mercy killing for Aruna Shaunbag, who had been in a vegetative state for 37 years, the Court established stringent guidelines for passive euthanasia under high-court monitoring. Close relatives, parents, or spouses of patients can approach the high court to seek passive euthanasia. Upon receipt, the Chief Justices of high courts constitute benches for evaluation, appointing committees of esteemed doctors for expert guidance. This landmark judgment reflects the evolving legal perspective on passive euthanasia in India and underscores the complex interplay of legal, ethical, and human rights considerations in the realm of end-of-life decisions.

7.   PSYCHIATRISTS' PERSPECTIVES ON VOLUNTARY EUTHANASIA IN INDIA

A significant concern raised pertains to the potential influence of depression on terminally ill patients' request for Physician-Assisted Suicide (PAS). Consequently, the involvement of psychiatrists becomes crucial in assessing depression in such patients. In certain jurisdictions, there is a legal mandate for mandatory psychiatric evaluation before granting permission for PAS. This role of psychiatrists is perceived as acting as gatekeepers in this contentious matter. However, concerns are also raised about the potential biases of psychiatrists in detecting depression in terminally ill patients, given the complexity of the situation.

Although the legalization of PAS remains of limited importance to the Indian legislature, a study conducted at the Central Institute of Psychiatry, Ranchi, aimed to gauge Indian psychiatrists' attitudes towards euthanasia, considering their potential role as gatekeepers in PAS decisions. The study involved 165 psychiatrists, with 99 completing the questionnaire. Interestingly, over 55% of participants favoured legalizing PAS, while only 28% opposed it. Factors influencing attitudes encompassed deeply ingrained moral values, the physician's role in preserving life, the potential to incentivize improved palliative care, religious beliefs, and resource allocation for palliative care. Furthermore, 60% expressed that they would consider PAS for themselves under terminal suffering. Criteria impacting their decision included pain (70%), absence of recovery prospects (50%), loss of mental faculties (49%), inability to self-care (35%), and diminished quality of life (35%). Surprisingly, 60% of respondents admitted uncertainty in diagnosing depression in terminally ill patients during a single interview, suggesting that personal moral principles and prior attitudes towards PAS might sway their decisions as future gatekeepers.

An additional survey conducted by the Society for the Right to Die with Dignity in Bombay encompassed 200 doctors, shedding light on the viewpoints of health professionals in India regarding euthanasia and PAS. Notably, 90% expressed awareness and concern about the topic, while 78% endorsed patients' right to choose in terminal illness cases. Seventy-four percent believed that artificial life support should not be prolonged when death is inevitable, yet only 65% indicated willingness to withdraw life support. Regarding Living Will, 41% believed it should be honoured, with 31% expressing reservations on the matter.

8.   ARGUMENTS IN FAVOUR OF EUTHANASIA

There has been lot of arguments held in favour of Euthanasia as a right to people supporting proponents of euthanasia, some of these arguments are:

➢   The argument supports that a person have a right to self-determination and should be allowed to choose his/her own fate.

➢   It has to be a better choice to die rather then they continue to suffer endlessly.

➢   Euthanasia as being into reality will not necessarily lead to any unacceptable consequences as with the reference of the countries like Netherlands and Belgium, the first mover of legalizing euthanasia, the Pro-Euthanasia Activists argue that the principle of euthanasia has been mostly unproblematic and as well helpful.

➢   Constitution of India: Right to Life as embodied into the ambit of Article 21, but euthanasia is still explained as an unnatural termination of life, therefore it is incompatible and inconsistent as with the provision of Article 21. This be the duty of the state to protect the life of the people and the duty of the physicians to provide care and not to harm patients. The Supreme Court of India in the Gian Kaur v. State of Punjab held that, the right to life under Article 21 does not include the right to die.

➢   Right to die supporters as well argue that patients who have an incurable, disabling or debilitating condition should be allowed to die in dignity. The majority of such petitions as filed are by the sufferers or their families or the caretakers. The caregiver's burden is also huge and it cuts across various domains such as financially, emotionally, physically, mentally and socially.

➢   The patients has an inherent right to refuse treatment, including the medical treatment that sustains or prolongs life. Recognition of the right to refuse treatment or deny it gives a way for passive euthanasia to excel.

➤ Euthanasia to be encouraged in terminally ill patients provides a wide opportunity as to advocate organ donation, which in turn would help a lot of patients as with organ failures waiting for transplant to survive. Euthanasia not only administers 'right to die' for patients with terminally ill conditions, but also 'right to life' for the organ needy patients.

9. ARGUMENTS AGAINST EUTHANASIA

There has been arguments against the legalization of euthanasia as a practice presented by the opponents of euthanasia, some of these arguments are as follows:

➤ First of all the opponents argue that, not all deaths are painful.

➤ Alternatives, such as cessation of active treatment, combined with the use of effective pain relief, are available.

➤ The distinction between passive and active euthanasia is morally more significant.

➤ Euthanasia if legalized in the state would place the society onto a slippery slope as believed by the opponents of euthanasia, which lead eventually lead to unacceptable consequences.

➤ Opponents believes that euthanasia will weaken the society's sanctity of life.

➤ Euthanasia might also not be always in the best interest of the person, as getting old parents killed for the property will.

➤ Opponents of euthanasia has a belief in God's miracle to cure the terminally ill patients.

➤ Certain Practical Arguments:

- Opponents of euthanasia argues to have no proper way of regulating euthanasia.

- Allowing euthanasia will eventually lead to less good care for the terminally ill.

- Euthanasia is allowed would lead to undermining of commitments of doctors and nurses saving lives.

- Euthanasia if allowed would discourage innovations in search for new cures and treatments.

10. LIVING WILL AND ATTORNEY AUTHORIZATION

In euthanasia, Living Wills and Attorney Authorization are legal tools expressing medical treatment preferences for those unable to communicate due to illness. These documents let individuals control decisions even when incapacitated.

A Living Will outlines treatment choices, like life-sustaining measures, if recovery is unlikely or quality of life diminishes. It guides medical and family choices. Attorney Authorization designates a healthcare agent to decide based on best interests and Living Will preferences. This trusted person could be a friend, family, or legal rep.

These documents aid end-of-life choices. If a person can't communicate, the Living Will guides treatment decisions. It legally supports euthanasia or assisted suicide based on expressed desires. These tools respect autonomy, reducing conflicts among family, caregivers, and medical staff. They contribute to the conversation on dignified end-of-life choices and ethical considerations.

11.   RELIGIOUS BELIEFS AND EUTHANASIA IN INDIA

With the religious beliefs being against the provision of premature death (euthanasia) held strong in India, right to life weighed greater than the right to die with dignity after the Supreme Court's verdict over the legal sanction of Euthanasia. The debate went on over and around issues related to legal, ethical, human rights, health-related etc. grounds. After the Supreme Court recognized the right to die with dignity as a fundamental right available to the patients, there were major hurdles posed by the religious communities who all were mostly opposing the decision regarding euthanasia in India.

In Hinduism Atma-gatha which means suicide explained as the intention to voluntary kill was prohibited in the Hindu Culture. With Hinduism, Muslims as well weren't in the favour of euthanasia though after the Supreme Court's verdict the community didn't made any public statements on the very subject and opposing the same. Under the Muslim law they believed that no one has a right to die before the time so decided by the God, the Mighty.

Be it Shias or Sunnis, according to both, killing a terminally ill person be it through active euthanasia or through passive euthanasia, is to be considered as a disobedience against the God and should be stood against to. Similar to their stand was the stand of Indian Christians, especially the Catholic Bishops Conference of India, was completely against the provision of euthanasia to be practiced. This was the statement released stating that, "Catholic Church forever promotes and supports the sanctity of life, thus euthanasia is contrary of its teachings".

Medical Professionals believes that passive euthanasia as a practice has been a common event in majority of hospitals across India where due to the huge cost involved in the treatment of the patients and the treatment to keep them alive as many poor terminally ill patients and their families withdrew their support (Passive Euthanasia). Euthanasia has come out as a necessity for the poor patients and their families and also the last resort as they can't afford the huge cost involved in the treatment to keep themselves or their loved ones alive, leaving them with no other choose then practicing euthanasia.

To help such a condition the Government has already started promoting palliative care policies for elderly, poor and terminally ill patients who are most likely and vulnerable to opt for euthanasia. This has been a belief of several religious entities and health officials that, "if we can provide the patients with good care and at an affordable price for the families then why would they opt for euthanasia snatching away the life of their loved ones".

This was the belief of Public Health experts that it is essential to assess the mental health status of the individual who is seeking for euthanasia as the main reason behind someone opting for euthanasia be depression, hopelessness, pain or lack or care. If these patients are taken care of then their decision can overcome that of euthanasia.

12.   JUDICIAL RESPONSE

India currently lacks any legislation that explicitly permits or validates mercy killing. The

241st Report of the Law Commission of India titled "Passive Euthanasia – A Relook" suggested the need for a law on passive euthanasia. This led to the drafting of The Medical Treatment of Terminally Ill Patients (Protection of Patients and Medical Practitioners) Bill, 2016. After being reviewed by experts, an expert committee proposed legislation for passive euthanasia.

The topic of mercy killing or euthanasia has raised legal and social concerns due to distressing situations. Some have argued that the right to die is encompassed within the right to life with dignity under Article 21 of the Indian Constitution. This viewpoint asserts that individuals facing prolonged suffering should be allowed to choose death to escape agony. While no specific legislation has been enacted by the Indian Parliament, the country's judiciary has interpreted euthanasia in various ways.

Initially, a Supreme Court bench stated that a person has the right not to live a coerced life and that attempted suicide is not illegal. However, this perspective was later overturned by a constitutional bench of the Supreme Court. Currently, passive euthanasia is legalized in India based on a decision by the apex judiciary.

Section 309 of the Indian Penal Code, which criminalized attempted suicide, was challenged for violating Articles 14 and 21 of the Indian Constitution. The argument was made that the right to life under Article 21 includes the right not to live or the right to die. The Supreme Court deemed Section 309 as harsh and irrational, and it was considered inhumane to penalize individuals already suffering due to their failure to commit suicide. The court concluded that the section should be removed from the statute book as it goes against public policy and morality without causing harm to society.

In the case of Airedale N.H.S. Trust v. Bland, it was emphasized that mercy killing isn't legally recognized under common law and can only be permitted through legislation. The case revolved around the withdrawal of life-sustaining measures from Anthony Bland, who had suffered brain damage and was in a persistent vegetative state due to injuries sustained during an assault. The House of Lords ruled that euthanasia is not sanctioned by common law and should only be authorized by legislation, particularly in situations where assisted suicide causes less suffering compared to the suffering that euthanasia is meant to alleviate. The principle of 'sanctity of life' was upheld.

In Gian Kaur, a challenge was made against the validity of section 306 of the Indian Penal Code, which penalizes abetting suicide. The case involved Gian Kaur and her husband Harbans Singh, who were convicted for abetting a suicide. The constitutional bench ruled that the right to life guaranteed under Article 21 of the Constitution does not encompass the right to die. The court differentiated between the natural right to life and the unnatural act of suicide, deeming them distinct and incompatible. The comparison between the right to life and the right to die was deemed unjustified due to Article 21 considerations. The constitutional bench upheld the constitutionality of sections 306 and 309 of the Indian Penal Code, asserting that euthanasia and assisted suicide are not lawful in India and should only be legalized through legislation.

In the Aruna Ramachandra Shanbaug v. Union of India , a writ petition was filed on behalf of a nurse who had been in a coma for 36 years after being raped in 1973. The petitioner sought permission to withdraw life-saving measures and feeding from the victim, arguing that this constituted passive euthanasia. However, the court denied the request after reviewing medical reports, considering stopping feeding as a form of passive euthanasia. The court emphasized that passive euthanasia could only be legalized in India through legislation.

In the recent case of Common Cause Society v. Union of India , the petitioner argued for the recognition of the right to die with dignity as a fundamental right under Article 21 of the Indian Constitution. They proposed the adoption of a "Living Will and Attorney Authorization" document that would allow individuals with deteriorated health or terminal illnesses to make decisions about their treatment. Passive euthanasia was supported as a way to relieve patients from unbearable suffering, and the concept of a living will was endorsed.

In today's context, advanced medical techniques can prolong life but may also subject patients to prolonged suffering. The right to self-determination should encompass the ability to choose or refuse treatment. When a patient is unable to express their wishes due to illness, they should be allowed to do so in advance through a living will or via a surrogate acting on their behalf. The court declared that the right to die with dignity is integral to society and that individuals with mental capacity have the right to refuse medical treatment, including withdrawing life-saving measures. The judgment also mandated the formation of committees to oversee these matters.

13.   CONCLUSION

As societal progress continues, the need to adapt and evolve laws becomes essential. The expansion of rights in various areas prompts the establishment of new legal dimensions. Previously, customs dictated much of the legal landscape, but even these have been refined through due process. Scientific and technological advancements introduce novel mechanisms, necessitating the recognition of new rights as well as their incorporation into statutory frameworks. Judicial decisions have also played a role in recognizing rights in the absence of legislation, as seen in the case of passive euthanasia.

Human life holds immense value, and preserving its sanctity remains paramount. While the state is obligated to ensure a secure and healthy life, modern complexities have introduced new challenges. Medical advancements have extended lives and offered relief, but they've also presented dilemmas, where individuals suffer amid prolonged existence. The right to lead a dignified life encompasses the right to self-determination, including the right to make choices about one's health. When patients face extreme suffering with no chances of recovery, the option to refuse treatment or choose passive euthanasia should be available. Such decisions should be handled with care, including psychiatric evaluation if necessary. Ensuring death with dignity aligns with the protection of human rights.

However, active euthanasia may not be currently suitable for India due to societal factors. The prevalence of crime, corruption, and property disputes underscores the need for comprehensive analysis before adopting such practices. The Supreme Court's decision to allow passive euthanasia is commendable, shedding light on an important issue. The court's focus on the patient's agony and peaceful departure resonates, and its decision expands the right to life under Article 21 of the Constitution. While the court's ruling is a positive step, it's now the responsibility of the Parliament to enact appropriate legislation and guidelines. This would provide clarity and structure in implementing passive euthanasia, while upholding the dignity and rights of individuals facing end-of-life challenges.

LIABILITY OF ROBOTIC AND AUTONOMOUS SYSTEMS

Authored by :- Pranay Nayak

Law Student at KLE Society's Law College

Technological progress and digital revolution have constantly challenged the common law system and the legal axioms that have been established and proved as an effective working system. The emergence of artificial intelligence and autonomous systems not only threatens to transform the various product markets but also threatens to challenge the laws governing these markets. Specifically, it summons **to contest the liability system prevalent in the torts law and the common law system.**

"Autonomous Systems", attributes to those systems that can make decisions and implement actions independent of human control. Within the robotics field there has been a huge transition from classical AI to Deep learning AI. While classical AI included multi-layered neural networks relying on symbolic logic to emulate 'natural thinking', deep learning AI utilizes these neural networks to establish a level of autonomy and the ability to learn from trained behavior. Using certain techniques like reinforcement learning, autonomous systems are able to do tasks, respond to situations without any human intervention and in doing so, they come up with solutions which are unpredictive in nature. Such self-learning programs have been used in software like language recognition and hardware systems like industrial robots and self-driven cars. Due to the self-learning techniques involved which control the behavior of the autonomous systems, **the issue of determining who is liable for any damages or unpredictable actions occurring is an important question that is placed in front of the courts.**

Identifying liability in autonomous systems

Liability under the tort law is basically a fault-based system, where one party owes the other party a duty of care. In case of any breach of duty, the party is said to be liable in tort and has to compensate the injured person. In the case of autonomous systems, it becomes difficult to identify the liability because they work on a black box system which involves a neural network whose decision-making complexity is sufficient that we cannot pinpoint a specific rule set that it can be governed by. An example for this is the **Toyota sudden acceleration lawsuits**, where the acceleration software built into the system went haywire and the passengers where unable to apply the brakes resulting in accidents. In the process of litigation, Toyota and the plaintiffs went through the source code of the acceleration software line by line looking for a defect but were unable to find the source of the issue. Although the blame was assigned to Toyota, it is this form of uncertainty that constitutes the difficulty in identifying liability in autonomous systems.

Liability requires a proof of damage and a causality link, that is, it is essential to prove that the damage incurred was caused by the act of harm, only then is the accused liable to pay compensation to the victim. In the example of a regular accident, where a car hits a bystander and injures him, we try to identify if the accident was caused by the negligence of the driver or by the failure of any mechanical part which may or may not have been in the control of the driver.

If this same case were to be an accident where, a self-driven car hits a bystander, then it would become very difficult to identify the person liable in this case. A number of parameters would have to be inspected, the causes for the accident could include the **negligence of the driver, the failure of a mechanical equipment, failure in the software written in the autonomous system**. It would be arduous to determine the exact source of the system failure in the source code, whether the driver could have undertaken certain steps to counter the system failure, whether the liability will fall into the hands of the manufacturer, developers or the auditing board who authorized the vehicle to run on the streets, whether a system of shares liability can be imposed.

Legal Challenges posed by autonomous systems

One of the primary reasons why identifying liability in case of autonomous systems is challenging is because of the various entities present in the blockchain of such systems. **First, the developer** who can be an individual or a large community of open source developers who can be anonymous, **second, the deployer** who takes the software, the budget and deploys it on the blockchain who again, can be anonymous, **third, the auditors or certification board**, who allow such a system to be employed in real world situations, **fourth, the users** who willingly interact with the autonomous system to achieve their purposes and finally the different entities who are participating to maintain the underlying blockchain and to ensure its execution. Even if the strenuous task of identifying the source of the issue is completed, it becomes very difficult to establish individual liability or shared liability.

Robots and autonomous systems are not recognized as persons or legal entities in the jurisdictions of most countries. **They are perceived as objects, which means that their actions are not attributed to themselves rather to the subjects responsible for them**. In most cases the subjects responsible for the objects would be the owners but in the case of autonomous systems there is no clear distinction between ownership and actual control. In most cases the entities exercising actual control could be anonymous.

Another concern regarding autonomous systems is if the existing laws are sufficient to accommodate the legal remedies or do new laws have to be established. In the current scenario the remedy is based on the type of harm caused, if the harm is **merely financial and economic** in nature it falls under the **realm of the contract law and the terms of use drawn up between the parties**, if the harm is **physical in nature**, it falls under the **realm of the tort law**.

With the increased employment of the autonomous systems in various fields, the incidents arising out of it will cause major conflict in the application of different statutes in the existing common law system.

The Society of Automotive Engineers (SAE) defines five levels of driving automation from fully manual to fully autonomous. According to this system, in level 1 the driver has complete control over the essential aspects like steering and accelerating. Level 2 operates advanced driver assistance systems where the vehicle controls both steering and accelerating but a human is on the driver's seat and can assume control at any point. Cruise systems are an example for level 2. Level 3 employs conditional driving automation where vehicles have 'environment detection' capabilities and can make decisions by themselves. In Level 4 automated machines do not need human intervention in most cases since they can intervene even in cases of system failure. Level 5 will be full driving automation where the complete control lies with the vehicle and it will produce the same results as an experienced driver.

Autonomous systems as a legal subject

One such proposed solution for identifying the liability in autonomous systems is to give the **autonomous systems the status of a legal entity and consider it an E-person who has civil liabilities.** In such a system, the burden of finding the party liable would fall away from the victims and on to the **robot's liability insurers**. These insurers would represent the legal entity of the autonomous systems would be inclined to investigate the facts, locate the source of system failure, and pose a credible threat to hold hardware manufacturers, software programmers, or users accountable in exercising their rights of recourse against them. The question is how to achieve a separate legal entity for autonomous systems without any incentives for the liability insurers.

Conclusion: Autonomous systems pose the ideal challenge of understanding the technological implications of multi layered autonomous systems and the legal understanding of the concepts and liability and establishing a working relation between the two. Our hope is to find systematic ways to fill up the gaps between the two entities and establish an efficient legal system governing the challenges that the rise of autonomous systems tends to pose.

1. Gerhard Wagner, "Robot, Inc.: Personhood for Autonomous Systems?" (2019) ,Pg 592,608.
2. Tarek Nakkach, "The liability of robotic and autonomous systems - available remedies for injury or damage caused by autonomous systems", (University of York, 21, October 2020) < https://www.york.ac.uk/assuring-autonomy/news/blog/liability-robotic-autonomous-systems-remedies/> accessed 15 July,2021.
3. "The 6 Levels of Vehicle Autonomy Explained", https://www.synopsys.com/automotive/autonomous-driving-levels.html
4. Herbert Zech, " Liability for autonomous systems: Tackling specific risks of modern IT", (University of Basel, May 1, 2018) accessed 16July, 2021.

BIBLIOGRAPHY

1. Art. 8, Rome Statute.

2. The Prosecutor v. Germain Katanga, ICC-01/04-01/017.

3. The Prosecutor v. Thomas Lubanga, ICC-01/04-01/06.

4. The Prosecutor v. Bosco Ntaganda, ICC-01/04-02/06.

5. https://www.theguardian.com/world/2022/mar/17/vladimir-putin-war-criminal- Ukraine-Russia-president-justice.

6. The Prosecutor v. Charles Ghankay Taylor, SCSL-03-01-A.

7. Specialist Prosecutor v. Hashim Thaçi, Kadri Veseli, Rexhep Selimi and Jakup Krasniqi, Case No. KSC-BC-2020-06.

8. The Prosecutor v. Omar Hassan Ahmad Al Bashir, ICC-02/05-01/09.

9. Article 7, Rome Statute.

10. Article 8, Rome Statute.

11. Article 6, Rome Statute.

12. Sloboden Milošević, Kosovo, Croatia & Bosnia, IT-02-54.

13. https://www.ohchr.org/en/press-releases/2022/10/un-commission-has-found-array- war-crimes-violations-human-rights-and.

14. https://www.europarl.europa.eu/RegData/etudes/BRIE/2022/733525/EPRS_BRI(2022)73 3525_EN.pdf.

15. https://www.ohchr.org/sites/default/files/documents/countries/ua/2022-09- 23/ReportUkraine-1Feb-31Jul2022-en.pdf.

16. https://www.icj-cij.org/public/files/case-related/182/182-20221019-WRI-01-00- EN.pdf.

"EMPOWERING CITIZENS: THE VITAL ROLE OF CONSTITUTIONAL EDUCATION IN MODERN SOCIETY"

Authored by:- Isha. Shailendra. Kakirde

Ramaiah College of Law- B.A. LLB

Abstract

Understanding our basic constitutional rights is essential for us as Indians as it gives us the power to exercise our freedoms, protect against unfair treatment, and promote a fair and just society. This article explores why being aware of these rights is so important, how it helps uphold our democracy, ensure social justice, and safeguard individual freedoms. It also highlights the need for education and information sharing to make sure that everyone of us not only knows our rights but can also stand up for them. In the end, informed citizens play a crucial role in holding those in power accountable, fostering democracy, and building a stronger, more inclusive nation.

Keywords: Constitutional Education, Empowerment, Democracy, Civil Rights.

Literature Review

1. In an article **titled "India Will Thrive Only When Its Citizens Are Aware of What Constitution Envisages,"**[1] Chief Justice of India (CJI) N V Ramana emphasized the vital role of constitutional education. CJI Ramana highlighted that a constitutional republic can thrive only when citizens are aware of their rights and duties as outlined in the Constitution. He urged law graduates to simplify constitutional provisions for the public, recognizing the law's potential for social change.

2. The article **titled "The Indian Constitution: Are You Informed or Ignorant About It?"** [2]sheds light on the crucial importance of constitutional awareness among Indian citizens. The article critiques the current state of constitutional education in schools, advocating for a more robust and comprehensive approach.

Furthermore, it emphasizes the significance of grasping fundamental rights, duties, and key constitutional principles, while also highlighting the distinction between acts and sections, the preamble's importance, and the constitution's salient features. The article stresses that such knowledge allows citizens to

---

[1](India Will Thrive Only When Its Citizens Are Aware Of What Constitution Envisages: CJI NV Ramana, July 31, 2022) (India Will Thrive Only When Its Citizens Are Aware Of What Constitution Envisages: CJI NV Ramana, July 31, 2022) (India Will Thrive Only When Its Citizens Are Aware Of What Constitution Envisages: CJI NV Ramana, July 31, 2022)

[2] Aakanksha Ahire, "The Indian Constitution: Are You Ignorant or Informed About It?" Youth Incorporated Magazine, August 17, 2022, https://youthincmag.com/the-indian-constitution-are-you-ignorant-or-informed about-it.

interpret the constitution positively and fosters a clear understanding of essential terms like sovereignty, secularism, justice, equality, fraternity, liberty, freedom, and integrity.

In summary, the article delves into the necessity for Indian citizens to be well informed about their constitution and its various aspects to promote responsible citizenship and peaceful coexistence in the country.

Research question

"How can constitutional education be effectively integrated into the Indian education system to ensure that citizens have a comprehensive understanding of their constitutional rights, duties, and the implications of key constitutional principles?"

By addressing this question, we can better understand how to promote constitutional awareness among the Indian populace, fostering responsible citizenship and harmonious coexistence.

Hypothesis

After a careful observation the writer's purpose is to disclose- as a citizen of India, it is necessary for each one of us to know our constitution. Of course, it's difficult to know every little detail about the world's longest written constitution, but we must know some crucial laws that govern our day-to-day lives.

Introduction

Education is a continual journey, serving as a preparation for the entirety of one's life. It represents the advancement of human existence, with society relying on its students as the bearers of this progress. Education plays a pivotal role in shaping a child's character and affords them the opportunities to pursue self-directed objectives. **As articulated by Gandhi," Education means all round drawing out of the best in child and man— body, mind and spirit "**[3]Education serves as the cornerstone for nurturing well rounded personalities, encompassing moral, intellectual, and emotional dimensions. Education is one of the key components that bring growth and progress into society. The more people in a society are educated, the more they can provide a beneficial contribution to the future of their country.

• **Constitutional education and its importance in contemporary society** [3]Tribune India, "By Education, I Mean an All-Round Drawing of the Best in Child and Man in Body, Mind and Spirit. — Mahatma Gandhi," *Tribuneindia News Service*, March 7, 2023, https://www.tribuneindia.com/news/thought-for-the-day/by-education-i-mean-an-all-round-drawing-of-the best-in-child-and-man-in-body-mind-and-spirit-%E2%80%94-mahatma-gandhi-485802.

Constitutional education at the same time is like a general knowledge which is crucial because it helps people understand the rules and values that guide a country. It's like a compass that shows us how to be responsible citizens and make society better. When we know our rights and duties, we can actively participate in our community and hold our leaders accountable. This knowledge also helps us respect the laws that keep our society fair and just.

Constitutional values are a vital resource for citizens, guiding them to understand and contribute to a harmonious society. To ensure the transmission of these values, it's essential to integrate them into school education through effective teaching methods, significant events, and projects aligned with the principles of the Indian constitution.

Studying constitutional values, citizen rights, and duties should be a compulsory subject at all levels of education, from primary to higher education. The constitution's preamble, which emphasizes social justice and equality through Articles 15, 16, and 17, highlights the importance of creating equal opportunities for all citizens. This foundational document, the preamble, holds the key to understanding the constitution's noble ideals and visions, making it a critical part of our educational curriculum.

Our educational institutions play a pivotal role in instilling these fundamental values in students, ensuring a brighter future for India. However, it's evident that students often lack awareness of constitutional values. While they may encounter these values through school activities, syllabi, and the recitation of the preamble, these exposures alone are insufficient. To bridge this gap, targeted programs are essential to cultivate a deep understanding and awareness of constitutional values among students.

How can we cultivate constitutional consciousness

• Developing a comprehensive understanding of the Indian Constitution is a vital endeavour, as it empowers individuals with knowledge about the fundamental principles and rights that underpin India's democracy. To embark on this educational journey, we can start by reading the Constitution itself, which is readily accessible online or in print. However, the pursuit of constitutional awareness extends beyond a mere perusal of the text; it involves actively engaging with various resources and avenues available for learning.[4]

• One effective way to familiarize ourselves with the Constitution is through educational institutions. Many schools and colleges in India include the study of the Indian Constitution as part of their curriculum, imparting foundational knowledge to students. • The internet is a treasure trove of resources for constitutional education. Numerous websites, educational platforms, and YouTube channels offer [4]

https://www.biicl.org/files/6646_burma_constitutional_awareness_booklet_-_english_version_(2).pdf understandable explanations, articles, and videos that break down the Constitution's complex provisions. Government websites, such as the National Portal of India, often feature comprehensive educational content related to the Constitution.

• Books and publications are the best resource for understanding our Indian constitution better. Books, publications, newspapers authored by renowned scholars and experts in constitutional law provide in-depth insights into the Constitution's nuances. These resources are valuable for those seeking a more profound understanding.

• Engaging with legal workshops, seminars, and webinars is another avenue for gaining constitutional knowledge. Various organizations, NGOs, and legal institutions organize such events, where experts delve into constitutional matters, provide historical context, and answer questions from participants.

• Online forums and social media groups dedicated to Indian law and governance foster discussions and debates on constitutional topics. Engaging in these discussions will help us practically understand our constitution better.

• With a practical active approach, we also have a visual approach. Visual learning, like documentaries and films that explore the Indian Constitution and its historical significance, watching such content can be both educational and engaging.

"By comprehensively exploring the Constitution through various resources, we can gain a multifaceted perspective and a deeper insight into its many dimensions."

Grasping the Essentials of Our Constitution: Foundational Insights.[5]

Constitution Day, observed on November 26th, is a significant occasion that marks the adoption of India's extensive Constitution. Every year on January 26th, Republic Day commemorates the moment when the Constitution came into effect in 1950. India takes pride in having the world's longest constitution, featuring a preamble, 22 sections housing 448 articles, 12 schedules, and having undergone 115 amendments. The preamble of India's Constitution proclaims the nation as a sovereign, socialist, secular, and democratic republic, with its fundamental objectives being justice, liberty, equality, and fraternity for all citizens, aimed at preserving India's unity and integrity. Notably, the original handwritten copies of the Constitution in both English and Hindi are meticulously preserved in the

[5] Aakanksha Ahire, "The Indian Constitution: Are You Ignorant Or Informed About It?," Youth Incorporated Magazine, August 17, 2022, https://youthincmag.com/the-indian-constitution-are-you-ignorant-or-informed about-it.

Central Library of the Indian Parliament. The monumental task of drafting this constitution spanned nearly three years and was masterminded by Dr. B.R. Ambedkar, who is rightly celebrated as the architect and father of the Indian Constitution. He assembled a seven-member 'Drafting Committee,' with himself as the Chairman. The other members of the committee included N. Gopalaswami, Alladi Krishnaswami Ayyas, K.M Munshi, Saijo Mola Saadulla, N. Madhava Rao, and D.P Khaitan. Our constitution is a mix of borrowings from the constitutions of various other countries that include the U.S., the U.K., France, Japan, Germany,[6] and the former Soviet Union (USSR). India's constitution is often described as a 'living constitution,' as it can be amended or modified to adapt to changing times, with new laws introduced and old ones discarded. Given India's multifaceted landscape, characterized by strong and diverse religious, cultural, and political ideologies, as well as challenges like intolerance, caste and gender

discrimination, and other social issues, constitutional awareness is paramount. This awareness is especially crucial for the youth, who are the future leaders of the nation, to acquaint themselves with, comprehend, and uphold our constitution. Only then can we collectively work towards fostering a positive, harmonious, and inclusive environment for all within our country.

What's in it for us?

Knowing our constitution offers a multitude of benefits, from safeguarding individual rights to fostering a more informed and engaged citizenry. It empowers us to assert our freedoms, hold authorities accountable, and actively participate in the democratic process. Constitutional knowledge is a cornerstone of social justice, ensuring equality for all, and promoting transparency and accountability in governance. It aids in conflict resolution, prevents the abuse of power, and supports the values of diversity and inclusivity. Ultimately, understanding our constitution strengthens the foundations of our democracy, contributing to a just and harmonious society where the rule of law prevails. Let us clearly understand it by few pointers Mainly it protects our rights, gives us legal literacy and helps us to know when our rights have been violated and when not

1. **Protection of Rights:** Understanding the constitution allows you to be aware of your fundamental rights and freedoms. This knowledge empowers you to exercise and protect your rights effectively.

2. **Legal Literacy:** Constitutional knowledge provides a foundation for legal literacy. It helps you understand the legal system, the rule of law, and the principles that guide the legal process.

3. **Cultural and National Identity:** Understanding the constitution can foster a sense of cultural and national identity. It helps citizens connect with the values and principles that our founding fathers sought to achieve

4. **Conflict Resolution:** Understanding the constitution can help resolve disputes and conflicts through legal means. It allows you to know when your rights have been violated and how to seek legal redress.

How constitutional awareness might save your life one day.

While knowing your constitution may not directly save your life in the same way that immediate medical intervention or personal safety measures can, there are situations where constitutional knowledge can be of vital importance in safeguarding your rights, well-being, and even indirectly contributing to your safety.

Scenarios where knowing the constitution can be of crucial importance:

1. **Protection of Civil Liberties:** In some cases, individuals may face wrongful arrest or arbitrary arrest or detention. Knowing your constitutional rights, such as in article 22 of the Indian Constitution which provides safeguards to the arrested person. Such as the right to remain silent, the right to legal representation, and protection against illegal searches and seizures, can prevent abuse of power by law enforcement and ensure a fair legal process.

2. **Freedom of Expression and Assembly:** In situations involving protests or public demonstrations, understanding your constitutional right to freedom of speech and assembly under article 19 of the Indian Constitution

3. **Due Process and Fair Trials:** If you are involved in legal proceedings, knowledge of your constitutional right to a fair trial (Article 6 of the Human Rights Act), access to evidence, and the right to confront witnesses can be critical in ensuring that justice is served. can help you peacefully advocate for your cause while avoiding unnecessary confrontations with authorities.

4. **Protection from Discrimination:** If you believe you are a victim of discrimination or unequal treatment, understanding constitutional provisions related to equal protection under the law can help you seek redress through legal means.

5. **Healthcare Decision-Making:** In some cases, individuals may face healthcare decisions that involve ethical and legal considerations. Familiarity with understanding of constitutional principles, such as the right to privacy (Article 21), can inform decisions related to medical treatment and end-of-life care.

6. **Environmental Protections:** Constitutional provisions related to environmental protections may include issues relating to clean air, clean water, and land use. Knowing these provisions can empower you to advocate for a healthy environment. Article 48-A of the constitution states that the state shall endeavour to protect and improve the environment and to safeguard the forests and wild life of the country.

7. **Access to Education and Public Services**: Constitutional rights related to education and access to public services can play a role in ensuring equitable access to essential resources and opportunities. The Constitution (Eighty-sixth Amendment) Act, 2002 inserted Article 21-A in the Constitution of India which provides that the State shall provide for free and compulsory education to all children of the age of six to fourteen years.

8. **Consumer and Property Rights** (exclusively under article 19 and 21): Understanding

property rights and consumer protections under the constitution can help you in disputes related to property ownership, contracts, or consumer rights.

While knowing the constitution won't directly save your life like immediate medical attention can, it can protect your rights, provide legal recourse in challenging situations, and contribute to your overall well-being and safety by ensuring that you are treated fairly and justly under the law. It empowers individuals to assert their rights and seek justice when necessary.

In Summary

In conclusion, having a strong knowledge of your country's constitution is not only a matter of civic responsibility but also a valuable and a vital tool for safeguarding your rights and your well-being. While it may not directly save your life in emergency situations, constitutional awareness plays an indispensable role in protecting your civil liberties, ensuring due process, and upholding principles of democracy. It empowers individuals to engage in civic life, hold authorities accountable, and seek justice when faced with legal challenges or situations where your rights were violated. Ultimately, constitutional knowledge contributes to a more just, equitable, and democratic society, where the rule of law prevails, and individual freedoms are respected and protected.

References

"Public Awareness Of Constitution". (january 27th, 2020). *The Hindu.*

Ahire, A. (August 17th 2022). The Indian Constitution : Are you Informed Or Ignorant About It? *Youth Incorporated Magzine.*

India Will Thrive Only When Its Citizens Are Aware Of What Constitution Envisages: CJI NV Ramana. (July 31, 2022). *outlookindia.*

DOWARY DEATH

AUTHORED BY :- GAURAV AGARWAL

OVERVIEW

Marriage in India is deeply rooted in traditions and cultural beliefs that have been passed down through generations. However, there is one custom that refuses to change - the dowry system. This system originated in medieval times when a gift, either in cash or kind, was given to the bride by her family to ensure her financial independence after marriage. During the colonial period, the British made dowry a mandatory practice, and it became the only legal way to get married.

A dowry refers to the transfer of parental property, gifts, or money at the time of a daughter's marriage. It differs from bride price or bride service, which are payments made by the groom or his family to the bride's parents. Dowry, on the other hand, involves the wealth transferred from the bride's family to the groom or his family, supposedly for the bride's benefit. Additionally, dower is the property settled on the bride herself by the groom during marriage, which she retains ownership and control over. In 1961, the Dowry Prohibition Act was enacted to prohibit the giving or taking of dowry and related offenses.

Dowry death, in 1986 a new offence know as dowry death was inserted in the IPC by the virtue of section 304-B. The provision under sec 304-B is more stringent than provided U/s 498-A of IPC

Dowry System in India

The practice of dowry in India involves the bride's family providing gifts or money to the groom, his parents, or his relatives as a condition for marriage. This custom originated from India's biased inheritance laws, which required amendments to prevent the unfair disinheritance of daughters. Dowry typically consists of cash, jewelry, household items like electrical appliances, furniture, bedding, and crockery, all of which help the newlyweds establish their home. The dowry system is known to place a significant financial burden on the bride's family. Unfortunately, in some cases, it also leads to crimes against women, ranging from emotional abuse to physical harm and even death. The payment of dowry has long been prohibited under specific Indian laws, including the Dowry Prohibition Act of 1961. Furthermore, Section 304-B and 498-A of the Indian Penal Code also address the issue of dowry.

The legal definition of dowry, as stated in the Dowry Prohibition Act, refers to a request for valuable property or security that is closely connected to the marriage. It is a form of consideration given by the bride's parents or relatives to the groom or his parents and guardians in exchange for agreeing to marry the bride.

Section 3 of the Dowry Prohibition Act of 1961 specifies that the penalty for giving or receiving dowry does not apply to gifts given during the wedding ceremony, provided that no demand for them has been made.

Despite the existence of laws against dowries in India for many years, they have been widely criticized for their ineffectiveness. The practice of dowry deaths and murders continues to occur without proper intervention in various parts of India, further highlighting concerns about enforcement. Section 498-A of the Indian Penal Code mandated automatic arrests of the groom and his family if the wife complains of dowry harassment. However, this law was often misused, leading to a Supreme Court ruling in 2014 that arrests can only be made with a magistrate's approval.

Causes of The Dowry

Various reasons have been suggested as cause of dowry practice in India. There include economic factors and social

Economic Factors

The system of dowry is influenced by various economic factors. These include inheritance systems and the economic status of the bride.

Some experts suggest that economic and legal factors, such as weak inheritance laws that favor sons, put women at a disadvantage when it comes to inheriting property. This leaves women reliant on their husbands and in-laws, who often keep the dowry when the marriage takes place. In an effort to address this issue, India passed the Hindu Succession Act in 1956, which granted equal legal rights to daughters and sons in Hindu, Sikh, and Jain families.

In theory, dowry provides women with economic and financial security in their marriage, through the provision of material goods. This helps to prevent the division of family wealth and offers a sense of security to the bride. Additionally, the dowry system can serve as a form of pre-mortem inheritance, as once a woman receives valuable gifts, she may be excluded from the family's estate. However, for many families, dowry has become a significant financial burden, often leading them to destitution due to excessive demands from the groom. The demand for dowry has also increased over time.

In terms of social factors, the value placed on marriage in certain regions reduces the likelihood of dowry being practiced, as the bride price system is more prevalent. In the northern parts of the country, marriages typically involve dowry.

In the southern regions of India, it is more customary for marriages to occur within the bride's family. This frequently involves close relatives or even distant cousins. Additionally, these unions often take place in closer proximity to the bride's family. Another significant aspect is that brides may have the opportunity to inherit land, which grants them greater control over their personal lives.

Despite the advancements in women's rights in India, women still find themselves in a subordinate position within their families. Factors such as education, income, and health significantly influence the dowry system and the level of independence a woman has in selecting her own spouse.

Types of Dowry crimes

Dowry is considered a major contributor towards observed violence against women in India. Some of these offences include physical violence, emotional abuses, and even murder of brides and young girls prior to marriage. The predominant types of dowry crimes relate to cruelty (which includes torture and harassment), domestic violence (including physical, emotional and sexual assault), abetment to suicide and dowry death (including, issues of bride burning and murder).

Cruelty

Cruelty in the form of torture or harassment of a woman with the objective of forcing her to meet a demand for property or valuable security is a form of dowry crime. The cruelty could be in the form of verbal attacks or may be accompanied by beating or harassment in order to force the woman or her family to yield to dowry demands. In many instances, the cruelty may even force the woman to commit suicide and it has been specifically criminalized by the anti-dowry laws in India.

Domestic violence

Domestic violence includes a broad spectrum of abusive and threatening behavior which includes physical, emotional, economic and sexual violence as well as intimidation, isolation and coercion. There are laws like the Protection of Women from Domestic Violence Act 2005 that help to reduce domestic violence and to protect women's rights.

Dowry murder

Dowry deaths and dowry murder relate to a bride's suicide or killing committed by her husband and his family soon after the marriage because of their dissatisfaction with the dowry. It is typically the culmination of a series of prior domestic abuses by the husband's family.

Most dowry deaths occur when the young woman, unable to bear the harassment and torture, commits suicide by hanging herself or consuming poison. Dowry deaths also include bride burning where brides are doused in kerosene and set ablaze by the husband or his family.

Sometimes, due to their abetment to commit suicide, the bride may end up setting herself on fire Dowry deaths can also include sex selective abortions and female feticide by parents who do not want to pay for their daughter's dowry when she comes of age. Daughters are often seen as economic liabilities due to the dowry system.

Dowry Death (Section 304-B)

Where the death of woman is caused by any burns of bodily injury or occurs otherwise than under normal circumstances within seven year of her marriage and it is shown that soon before her death she was subjected to cruelty or harassment by her husband or any relative of her husband for, or in connection with any demand for dowry, such death shall be called Dowry Death, and such husband or relative shall be deemed to have caused her death.

Whoever commits dowry death shall be punished with imprisonment for a term which shall not be less than seven years but which may extend to imprisonment for life.

Explanation

For the purpose of this sub-section, Dowry shall have the some meaning as in section 2 of the dowry prohibition Act, 1961.

Essential Ingredients

Death of woman should be caused by burns or bodily injury nor otherwise under normal circumstances.

Death should have been occurred within 7 years of her marriage.

The woman must have been subjected to cruelty or harassments by her husband or any relative of her husband.

Such cruelty or harassments should be or in connection with, any demand for dowry.

Such cruelty or harassment should have been subjected soon before her death.

It death of women caused under the above circumstance, the husband and husband's relative will be presumed to have caused a dowry death and be liable for the offences, unless it is proved otherwise.

Punishment

Under section 304-B (2) of IPC whoever commits dowry death shall be punished with imprisonment for a terms which shall not be less than 7 yrs. but which may extend to imprisonment for life.

Classification of Offence
The offence U/s 304-B is
Cognizable

Nonbailable

Non- compoundable

Tribal by Court of Session

Dowry Death and Evidence Act, 1872
Section 113-B presumption as to dowry death

When the question is whether a person has committed the dowry death of a woman and it is shown that soon before her death such woman had been subjected by such person to cruelty or harassment for, or in connection with any demand for dowry. The court shall presume that such person had caused the dowry death.

Explanation
For the purpose of this section Dowry Death Shall have the same meaning as in section 304-B of IPC.

SherSingh @ partapa v/s State of Haryana
A two judge bench [Vikramjit Sen and Kurian Jospe Joseph JJ] of the SC while dealing with section 304-B

IPC and section 113-B Evidence Act held as follows:

The prosecution can discharge the initial burden to prove the ingredients of section 304-B even by preponderance of probabilities.
Once the presence of the concomitants are established or shown or proved by the prosecution, even by preponderance of possibility, the initial presumption of innocence is replaced by an assumption

of guilt of the accused, thereupon, Transferring the heavy of proof upon him and requiring him to produce evidence dislodging his guilt, beyond reasonable doubt.

Case Laws

Hansraj V. State of Punjab
In this case SC held that term normal circumstances apparently mean not by natural death.

Rameshwar Das V. State of Punjab, 2008
In this case Sc held that, pregnant women, woman would not commit suicide unless relationship with her husband comes to such a passed that she would be compelled to do so, accused is liable to be convicted on the failure to prove his defense.

Dowry Prohibition Act, 1961

Section 2 Definition of **Dowry**

In this act, dowry means any property or valuable security given or agreed to be given either directly or indirectly.

By one party to a marriage to the other party to the marriage, or by the parents of either party to a marriage or by any other person.

To either party to the marriage or the any other person at or before or any time offer the marriage in connection with the marriage of said parties but does not include dowry or mahr in the case of persons to whom the Muslim personal law (Shariat) applies.

Case Laws

Satyanandam v/s Public Prosecutor, High Court of A.P.,2004
In this case court held that where the offence of dowry death is not proved the accused can still be convicted for dowry demand.

State of Andhra PradeshV.Ram Gopal Asawa & Another (AIR 2004 SCC 470)
In this case court held that there must be proximate and live link between the effects of cruelty based on dowry demand and the concerned death.

Kans Raj v/s State of Punjab, AIR 2000 SC 2324
For the fault of the husband, the in-laws or the other relations cannot, in all cases, be held to be involved in the demand of dowry. In cases where such accusation is made, the overt acts attributed to persons other than husband are required to be proved beyond reasonable doubt. By mere conjectures and implications such relations cannot be held guilty for the offence relating to dowry death. A tendency has however developed for roping in all relations of the in-laws of the deceased wives in the matters of dowry death which, if not discourage is likely to affect the case of the prosecution even against the real culprits. In their over enthusiasm and anxiety to seek conviction for maximum people the parents of the deceased have been found to be making efforts for involving other relations which ultimately weaken the case of the prosecution even against the real accused as appears to have happened in the instant case.

Arnesh Kumar v/s State of Bihar, 2014 (8) SCC 273

There is a phenomenal increase in matrimonial disputes in recent years. the institution of marriage is greatly revered in this country. Section 498-A IPC was introduced with avowed object to combat the menace of harassment to a woman at the hands of her husband and his relatives. The fact that section 498-A IPC is a cognizable and non-bailable offence has lent it a dubious place of bride among the provisions that are used as weapons rather than shield by disgruntled wives. The simplest way to harass is to get the husband and his relatives arrested under these provisions. In a quite number of cases, bedridden grandfathers and grandmothers of the husband, their sisters living abroad for decades are arrested.

Conclusion

The dowry at present is source of both joy and curse in the society. it is also a joy to the husband and his relatives who get cash, costly dress and utensils, furniture, bedding materials, etc.

But, it is a curse to the bride's parents who have to bear enormous cost to satisfy the unreasonable demands of the bridegroom's party. a demand of dowry does not diminish even after marriage. in some instances, the in-laws of the bride are very much ready to inflict harassment, insults and tortures both mental and physical.

It is often seen that, when more pressure is put on bride's parents, their dear daughter has no other option but to commit suicide to avoid more insult and torture at the hands of the members of her husband's family moreover, when deaths occur through bride burning, evidence itself is usually lost in flames.

GENDER EQUALITY UNDER THE INDIAN LEGAL SYSTEM

Authored by - Ajmi S & Hamsa Wadigera
B.A LLB
Ramaiah College of law

ABSTRACT

Gender equality means that people of all genders are free to pursue any career, lifestyle, or abilities they desire, regardless of their gender. The Universal Declaration of Human Rights, adopted on December 10, 1948, by the United Nations General Assembly, incorporated it into international human rights law. Gender inequality leads to unequal opportunities across India, and while both genders are affected, women are statistically the most disadvantaged. Although our constitution plays a pioneering role in ensuring gender equality, it is doubtful how effective it is in preventing gender discrimination. The primary aim of this article is to look into various provisions and legal frameworks in India enacted to prevent gender inequality. It also sheds light on various challenges hindering the goal of gender equality. This article also gives an understanding of the effectiveness of the legal safeguards against gender inequality pointing out some of the major problems. It also provides some possible measures that can be taken to prevent the gender gap. Furthermore, it gives a comprehensive picture of India's standing on gender equality. But in the efforts to achieve the goal of gender inequality, is India favoring women over men? It's time we brought in the concept of gender- neutrality in society.

– Keywords: *gender equality, gender inequality, discrimination, women, men*

INTRODUCTION

Gender equality implies having equality in rights, responsibilities, and opportunities, access to resources, political and economic participation, and decision-making among genders. Everyone is affected by gender inequality such as women, men, trans, gender diverse people, children, and families. There persists a worldwide gender gap and India is no exception. Gender equality is an important factor in the overall development of any country. Also, achieving the goal of gender equality is no easy task, but, the important steps that can be taken to this concern involve promoting equal respect for all genders, actions against sex trafficking, femicide, gender pay gap, etc. In this modern era, practices of gender equity and gender neutrality have shown quite a progress in society. It is also to be noted that there have been several initiatives developed to estimate gender inequality across the world, This involves the Gender Inequality Index by the United Nations Development Programme, and the Global Gender Gap Index by the World Economic Forum among others, which statistically indicate gender disparity collecting information of various gender discrimination in various aspects. This has been a very operative tool in tackling gender inequality among countries and helping them to look into the problems and improve their standing globally. Such schemes have an unquestionable impact on the political, social, and economic advancement of the world.

Gender equality in India is defined as having equal access to enough resources and opportunities regardless of gender, as well as equally valuing different behaviors, desires, and needs. It's all about being on an equal footing in all aspects of life. Gender equality is a fundamental human right and a necessary foundation for a world that is peaceful, wealthy, and sustainable. Despite its efforts and numerous legal frameworks, India continues to lag behind many other countries in achieving gender equality.

GENDER EQUALITY AND CHALLENGES IN INDIA

Gender inequality in India is a complex topic that has affected both men and women in the past and present. In India, numerous forms of gender inequality emerge for a variety of causes. Gender disparity in Indian society is rooted in the patriarchal system, which discriminates against women in areas such as education, health, choice, and labor. The male-dominated society's view of gender roles has kept women from progressing. Another important factor contributing to gender inequality is discrimination against girls and a preference for sons, who are deemed more useful than girls. As a result, boys are given exclusive rights to inherit the family name and property, and they are viewed as a status symbol for their family. Countless women are forced to work in low-paying domestic services, organized prostitution, or as migratory laborers as a result of poverty and a lack of education. The practice is common across all regions, classes, and religions. In India, the dowry system leads to gender inequality by instilling in families the belief that females are a burden. Women have likewise been maintained on a lower level than men. India has witnessed several women's movements and protests against gender discrimination. The history of India has been furnished with numerous reforms for the upliftment of women and has created a huge impact in tackling the problem of gender equality but still, there has not been a complete eradication of gender inequality and the problems continue. If women in the past were subjected to issues of illiteracy, labor participation, etc., the women of the present modern period are exposed to discrimination in workplaces. Apart from these, the other challenges hampering India from attaining gender equality involve, lack of access to credit, gender-based violence, lack of awareness, etc. contributing to gender inequality.

Despite continuous performance on gender equality, the country's legal ranking in this area has dropped to 124th out of 190 nations in 2022, according to World Bank research, showing that there is still a long way to go. Gender inequality is particularly terrible not just because it denies women access to basic social opportunities, but also because it jeopardizes future generations' lives.

LEGAL AND CONSTITUTIONAL SAFEGUARDS FOR GENDER EQUALITY

The Preamble to the Indian Constitution outlines the goals of establishing social, economic, and political justice for all people, as well as giving equality of position and opportunity to everyone. In terms of Articles, Acts, and other State initiatives, there are numerous frameworks.

- Constitutional Articles:

Article 14 ensures equality before the law, Article 15 outlaws discrimination based on sex, as well as other criteria like religion, race, caste, and place of birth, and Article 15(3) authorizes the state to make any specific provision for women and children. Article 16 grants equality of opportunity for all citizens in matters relating to employment or appointment to any office under the State. Furthermore, the Directive Principles of State Policy include several provisions that benefit women and provide safeguards against discrimination, such as the right to an adequate means of livelihood for both men and women (Article 39(a)) and equal pay for equal work for both men and women (Article 39(d)).

- Legal Provisions under the Indian Penal Code of 1860:

The major crimes identified under the Indian Penal Code (IPC) 1860, which primarily aims to protect women include:

- Rape (Sec. 376 IPC)
- Kidnapping & Abduction for different purposes (Sec. 363-373)
- Homicide for Dowry, Dowry Deaths, or their attempts (Sec. 302/304-B IPC)
- Torture, both mental and physical (Sec.498-A IPC)
- Molestation (Sec. 354 IPC)
- Acid attack (Section 326A)
- Act with intent to disrobe a woman (Section 354B)
- Sexual Harassment (Sec. 509 IPC)

- Acts:

The parliament also ensures that various acts are brought in the best social interest of preventing discrimination between genders, eliminating exploitation of women, and giving them equal status in society. Such legislations include The Sati (Prevention) Act 1987 was enacted to abolish and make punishable the inhuman custom of Sati and The Dowry Prohibition Act 1961 to eliminate the practice of dowry. The Special Marriage Act 1954 provides rightful status to married couples who marry inter-caste or inter-religion. The Pre-Natal Diagnostic Techniques (Regulation and Prevention of Misuse) Bill (was introduced in Parliament in 1991) and passed in 1994 to stop female infanticide. These are some of the major milestone legal provisions that were enacted against gender inequality. Apart from these are many other Acts such as The Prohibition of Child Marriage Act 2006, The Equal Remuneration Act 1976, The Medical Termination of Pregnancy Act 1971, and The Protection of Women from Domestic Violence Act 2005 among others.

However, laws that are exclusive to women, often implemented as a means of addressing gender disparities and historical injustices, can have various effects on men. It's important to note that these laws are typically introduced to promote gender equality and correct historical imbalances. However, they can lead to concerns or unintended consequences for men. To state a few examples, The Rape in IPC starts with A 'Man' is said to commit "rape" if he:......

In this, it's important to understand that according to IPC rape is only committed by men against women. This gender-specific language has been criticized for not recognizing the possibility of men being victims of rape and women being perpetrators. Sec. 354B of the IPC addresses the use of criminal force against women with the intent to disrobe them. While the intention behind such legal provision is to protect the dignity and modesty of women, if they had made it gender-neutral there would be no less protection to women. Sec 509 of IPC also talks about sexual harassment to women only. But in the 21st century, even a man can be sexually harassed but the irony is there is no provision to protect men from sexual harassment.

The Office for National Statistics figures show every year that one in three victims of domestic abuse is male equating to 699,000 men in 21/22 (1.671m women). One in 6-7 men and one in 4 women will be a victim of domestic abuse in their lifetime.

It's crucial to recognize that these laws are often introduced to correct gender imbalances and promote gender equality. Addressing potential concerns or unintended consequences should involve a balanced approach that ensures the rights and opportunities of all individuals, regardless of gender. Gender-neutral policies and ongoing debates can help achieve this balance.

ARE THESE LEGAL FRAMEWORKS ENOUGH?

In India, there exist suitable laws and frameworks that address gender discrimination and empower women but, in a male-dominated society, the Constitution allows for discriminatory laws in favor of women, who are regarded as the weaker sex, disadvantaged, and discriminated against. The government's action plan for combatting discrimination has proven the laws to be ineffective. In India, the fact that these laws only exist in books is a huge issue. The Supreme Court, on the other hand, has taken action and, in some situations, issued directives to the government. For instance, in the case of *C.B. Muthamma v. Union of India & Ors*, the apex court curbed the gender inequality that prevailed in the Indian Civil Service.

However, to eliminate discrimination in society, these laws must be implemented in a practical sense. The majority of the clauses of the IPC that deal with crimes against women solely refer to men as criminals. Some laws favor women over men like Rape, Alimony in Divorce, etc. But when we talk about equality we should have gender-neutral laws inclusive of men, women, and even the LGBTQ+ community. It is a fall of a legal system that favors women and its potential transformation into one that disadvantages other genders in a complex and contentious topic. One of the major steps taken towards gender neutrality by the Supreme Court is decriminalizing the offense of adultery which is highly gender-biased towards women. In the year 2018, in the case of *Joseph Shine v. UOI*, it was decriminalized by the Supreme Court. It's important to note that the goal of legal systems should ideally be to ensure gender equality, rather than favoring one gender over another. However, there have been instances where certain legal provisions or societal attitudes have been perceived as biased in favor of women. Therefore, it's time to bring effective reformations.

CONCLUSION

Gender equality's primary purpose is to create a society where men and women have equal opportunities, fairness, and responsibilities at all stages of life. When men and women share power and influence equally, equality emerges. Gender equality is crucial for India's growth from all perspectives. The central government has articulated several progressive steps to improve gender equality in social, economic, and political arenas in the last few decades, and policies relating to women's rights have had a favorable trajectory. Inequality between men and women exists in all aspects of life, including education, economic opportunity, representation in government, and other public and private institutions. Both men's and women's efforts would be able to develop answers to the problem of gender disparity, leading us all closer to our cherished dream of a completely contemporary society in both thinking and action, as well as political inequities between men and women in India. The demands of the day are trends in which girls are able not only to break free from culturally set patterns of employment but also to offer guidance on career options that extend beyond the usual list of jobs. It is astonishing that, despite numerous rules, women continue to face tension and strain.

But at the same time, Men in Indian society face exploitation through various societal pressures and gender stereotypes. Traditional expectations of being the primary breadwinner and conforming to rigid notions of masculinity can lead to stress and emotional burdens. Additionally, men may encounter biases in legal matters, reluctance to seek help for mental health issues due to stigma, and even domestic violence, though it is often underreported. Addressing these challenges requires promoting a more inclusive and equitable society where individuals of all genders are free from the constraints of harmful stereotypes and societal pressures. Long-term solutions can increase their strength and serve as a road map for their transformational and lifelong chances. We still have a long way to go to achieve gender equality.

UNIFORM CIVIL CODE AND ITS IMPORTANCE

Authored by- Gautam Choudhary

Introduction

The concept of a Uniform Civil Code (UCC) in India embodies the aspiration for a standardized legal framework that would be applicable to all citizens, irrespective of their religious affiliations, in matters concerning marriages, divorces, adoptions, and inheritance. It seeks to replace the divergent personal laws rooted in religious scriptures, statues, and customs that have long shaped the legal landscape in the country. In today's progressive era, characterized by a move towards inclusivity and equality, biases based on religion, class, caste, and gender are increasingly being challenged. In this context, the notion of a secular community where discriminatory opinions and thinking have no place gains significance. Secularism is a vital aspect that underpins the drive for uniformity, as represented by the UCC. Yet, the implementation of a UCC remains a contentious topic in India, marked by resistance from various religious groups, particularly Muslim communities.

Historical Background

The historical foundations of the UCC can be traced back to colonial India, during which the British government recognized the need for codifying Indian laws, including those concerning contracts and crimes. Notably, the British government suggested excluding the personal laws of Hindus and Muslims from this codification. As the colonial era progressed, there was a growing legislative focus on personal issues, which culminated in the formation of the B.N. Rau Committee in 1941. This committee was tasked with the codification of Hindu Law, an effort aimed at examining the need for common Hindu laws. The resulting codification, in accordance with scriptural tenets, introduced provisions that granted women equal rights. Furthermore, the Hindu Succession Act of 1956 represented a significant milestone, granting greater property rights to women, particularly within the context of inheritance.

Impact on Hindu Law

The Hindu Succession Act of 1956, influenced by the recommendations of the Rau Committee, addressed the concerns of inheritance among Hindus, Buddhists, Jains, and Sikhs. The Act sought to rectify gender imbalances and inequalities that had long characterized Hindu personal laws. Key amendments introduced in 2005 further enhanced the rights of female heirs, ensuring that daughters were entitled to the same share of inheritance as sons. However, it's important to note that separate personal laws continued to be applicable to other religious communities such as Parsis, Christians, and Muslims.

Article 44 and the Directive Principles

The foundation of a UCC rests on Article 44 of the Indian Constitution, which is a part of the Directive Principles of State Policy. Article 44 calls for the state's efforts to secure for its citizens a uniform civil code throughout the country. Despite more than six decades since its incorporation, the implementation of a UCC has remained elusive. Article 44 was introduced with the aim of achieving a balance between protecting the rights of vulnerable groups and fostering cultural cohesion. During the process of framing the Constitution, Dr. B.R. Ambedkar articulated the desirability of a UCC that was voluntary in nature. While Article 44 embodies this vision, other articles, namely Articles 25-28, grant Indian citizens the freedom to practice and manage their religious affairs independently. Thus, Article 44 stands as a directive principle, leaving it to the government's discretion to enact relevant laws.

Importance of a Uniform Civil Code

The necessity for a UCC is underscored by several factors. In a modern world that emphasizes equal rights for all citizens, the promotion of gender equality, the alignment of young minds with progressive thought, and the fostering of national integration are paramount.

Achieving these objectives necessitates a UCC that transcends the centuries-old dominance of men over women. While the British colonial rulers codified various laws related to contracts, property, and crimes, they refrained from intervening in religious and cultural matters. As a result, personal laws pertaining to marriage, family, and inheritance persisted largely unchanged. The inclusion of Article 44 in the Constitution represented a forward-looking perspective, anticipating the eventual
implementation of a UCC. However, this vision has yet to be fully realized even after more than six decades.

A Global Perspective

A compelling point of consideration is that almost every country, except India, has a uniform civil code applicable to all citizens. The implications of a UCC go beyond mere legal standardization. When effectively enforced, it has the potential to eliminate discrimination based on religious beliefs. A significant concern in this regard is the suppression of women's rights within religious contexts. A prime example of this is the Mohd. Ahmed Khan v. Shah Bano case. In this landmark case, the Supreme Court ruled that a divorced Muslim woman was entitled to maintenance under Section 125 of the Code of Criminal Procedure, 1973, even after the completion of her iddat period. However, the subsequent political response and enactment of controversial laws underscore the tension between personal laws and gender equality.

Equal Treatment and the Principle of Uniformity

A fundamental principle underlying a UCC is the guarantee of equal treatment for all citizens, irrespective of their religious affiliations. Article 14 of the Indian Constitution enshrines the concept of equality before the law and the courts. However, existing legal frameworks based on religion create a paradox wherein individuals of different faiths are subjected to dissimilar laws. For instance, while a Muslim man is permitted to have multiple wives without legal consequences, individuals from other religions face legal sanctions for practicing similar actions. This incongruity reflects a lack of true equality and highlights the imperative for a UCC that addresses such disparities comprehensively.

Modernization and Eradication of Discrimination

The implementation of a UCC holds the potential to usher in an era of modernization and eradicate caste and religious agendas from politics. While India has made significant strides in economic development, it still lags behind in certain aspects of social progress. The social fabric of the nation stands at a crossroads, straddling the fine line between modernity and tradition. A UCC could provide the impetus for India to reclaim its position as a socially and culturally vibrant nation, free from the shackles of discrimination.

Empowering Women and Ensuring Rights

Women have historically been subjected to subjugation and domination in many societies, including India. The implementation of a UCC could serve as a powerful tool for women's empowerment, enabling them to stand shoulder to shoulder with men in all spheres of life. The rights of women have been curtailed by religious laws, regardless of the faith they belong to. For instance, the issue of triple talaq in Islam has sparked significant debates, with Muslim women advocating for their rights against the backdrop of personal laws that often deny them equality. Dr. B.R. Ambedkar's advocacy for Hindu women further underscores the urgency of implementing a UCC to address the myriad challenges faced by women across religious communities.

Balancing Secularism and Cultural Diversity

The UCC hinges on the principles of secularism and cultural diversity. While secularism is a foundational aspect of Indian democracy, interpretations of this concept vary. Consequently, the UCC is both championed and criticized, depending on one's perspective. Some argue that the UCC stands as a potential threat to secularism, while others view it as a conduit for fostering communal harmony and preserving the essence of secular principles. However, the rights of Indian women are an underlying concern, hovering in the background of this debate.

Potential Impacts of a Uniform Civil Code

The present absence of a UCC raises questions about its potential impact on society. While its implementation is uncertain, its significance cannot be underestimated. The secular foundation of the UCC promotes coexistence, emphasizing the importance of harmonious living regardless of religious beliefs. Secularization goes beyond the exclusion of religious matters, extending to areas such as family laws, marriage, and inheritance. The contentious issue of triple talaq, for instance, has reignited the debate surrounding the UCC's implementation, with some advocating for its adoption to safeguard the rights of Muslim women.

Social Evolution and Family Dynamics

The implications of a UCC extend to social evolution and family dynamics. The absence of a UCC has allowed individuals to marry multiple partners, leading to larger families with children who often grow up without the active involvement of fathers. Implementing a UCC could potentially encourage more responsible family planning and active participation of fathers in child-rearing. In a society where family structure significantly influences overall development, a UCC could contribute to a more civilized and educated citizenry, thereby facilitating societal and national progress.

Modernization through a Uniform Civil Code

The introduction of a UCC holds the promise of modernization for India. It serves as a symbol of change and transformation, impacting various aspects of society. The modernization brought about by a UCC extends beyond legal standardization; it encompasses the empowerment of women, the transformation of family dynamics, and the upgradation of social standards. As India endeavors to balance tradition and progress, a UCC could become the catalyst for aligning the nation with global norms and values.

Challenges and Divergent Perspectives

Despite the compelling rationale for a UCC, challenges persist in its implementation. Opposition from various quarters stems from differing perspectives and concerns. Some individuals resist the idea due to misunderstandings or apprehensions, while others perceive it as a potential threat to their religious identity. The apprehension that a UCC might undermine religious customs and beliefs underscores the need for nuanced communication and dialogue around this topic. Additionally, political dynamics play a role, with some parties exploiting religious sensitivities to secure their interests.

Conclusion:

In conclusion, a UCC is not merely a legal reform but a manifestation of India's collective journey towards a more unified and inclusive future. The nation's rich cultural heritage and diverse religious landscape demand an approach that respects individual faith while ensuring equal treatment under the law. The pursuit of a UCC encapsulates the ideals of justice, equality, and

modernization. While it is imperative to address concerns and apprehensions, the larger goal of a UCC aligns with the principles of a progressive and harmonious society. As India navigates the complexities of tradition, modernity, and diversity, the implementation of a UCC could stand as a beacon of change, signaling a new era of equality and unity for the nation.

References

- Lawteacher.net
- Legalserviceindoa.com
- India.com
- Ijarnd.com
- Business-standard.com

FINANCIAL EXCLUSION OF WOMEN IN UNORGANISED WORKFORCE

Authored by:- **YASH RAWAT**

INTRODUCTION

Access to fiscal services gives openings for generating income, accumulating means, and sharing further completely in profitable conditioning, thereby promoting social and profitable commission. fiscal addition also offers adaptability from shock events like the COVID- 19 epidemic, which stressed the need for icing that the poorest populations have access to formal fiscal services. For women, in particular, fiscal addition is an necessary thing. exploration indicates that fiscal addition has a positive impact on women's control over ménage coffers by adding their savings. Yet encyclopedically, women continue to face walls to penetrating fiscal services. Data from the Global Findex Database 2021 shows that women and the poor are more likely to warrant evidence of identity or a mobile phone, live far from a bank branch, and need support to open and effectively use a bank account.

India, in 2014, launched the Pradhan Mantri Jan Dhan Yojana(PMJDY) to promote fiscal addition in every ménage in the country. The end of the action is to give the ' financially barred ' access to fiscal services similar as introductory savings bank accounts, need- grounded credit, remittances installation, insurance, and pension. Since also, according to data from the Ministry of Finance, over 460 million bank accounts have been opened 67 percent of them are in the pastoral andsemi-urban sections, and 56 percent are possessed by women. The average deposit quantum in PMJDY accounts has increased by nearly three times, from INR,279 in 2015 to INR,761 in 2022. still, nearly 20 percent of women in India remain without access to a bank account. Among those who do have a bank account, there are gaps in use of similar accounts, and they also continue to warrant access to savings and credit.

The imperative is for these gaps to be filled, as fiscal addition is recognised as a crucial motorist of profitable growth and poverty relief. It ensures universal access to useful and affordable fiscal services delivered in a responsible and sustainable manner. The Reserve Bank of India, releasing the National Strategy for Financial Addition(2019- 2024), defined ' fiscal addition ' as " the process of icing access to fiscal services and timely and acceptable credit where demanded by vulnerable groups similar as weaker sections and low- income groups at an affordable cost. The rest of this brief analyses the gender gaps in fiscal addition in India. It utilises literature review, consultations with experts, and data sets from the Global Findex Database 2021, the rearmost rounds of the National Family Health Survey 2019 – 21, and the All- India Debt and Investment Survey 2019, to present current substantiation on the gender peak. The brief underlines the eventuality of digital services in closing the gap.

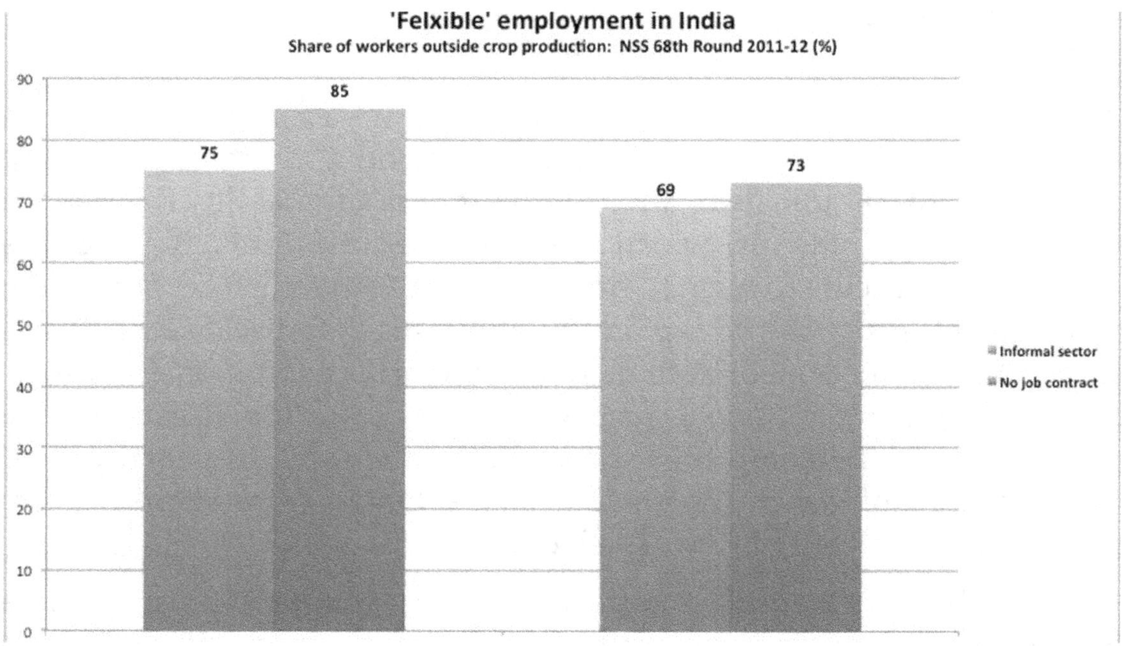

The Context: Findex Study 2021,

Women Left Behind in the Global Landscape

The World Bank's Global Findex Database compiles information on the availability of financial services worldwide, including payments, savings, and borrowing. The 2021 edition includes indicators on access to the usage of formal and informal financial services as well as digital payments. It polled 128,000 individuals in 123 economies during the COVID-19 pandemic.

According to the NFHS-5, only 38.3% of urban women and 45.7% of rural women individually or jointly own a home or piece of land. Female labour force participation rate (FLFPR) is much lower than male labour force participation rate, according to the Centre for Monitoring Indian Economy (CMIE) research. Male LPR was 66% between January and April 2022, while FLFPR was 9%. While the LPR for men in the 25–59 age range consistently exceeds 90%, the FLFPR has never fallen below 20% for any age range. It is imperative to support a safety net for women that can guarantee their participation in the labour force. Yet, the government is taking a number of steps.

According to a report on the financial inclusion of women by Micro Save Consulting (Nov 2019), 77% of Indian women now have access to financial services, compared to just 14% three years ago (before 2014). This action was applauded and recognised widely. Nevertheless, digging further into the Findex data revealed the depressing finding that 42% of the 77.5% of women have inactive profiles. About two thirds (65%) of women overall do not have an account, and 42% of those who have have dormant accounts. The fact that 35% of women actively using accounts at banks, post offices, or other financial institutions also include proxy users

Our Goals for Women's Financial Inclusion:-

A bit more than half of the world's population are women, but they contribute far less than they could to measurable economic activity, growth, and well-being, which has enormous macroeconomic repercussions. Comparatively, three-quarters of men and less than half of women over the world work. Up to 95% of women are employed in informal jobs in underdeveloped countries, where they are not covered by social security or labour laws. Missed possibilities for people, households, and economies are a result of this inequality. The expansion of businesses, the production of assets for households, and self-employment all depend on the availability of financial services. The inability of women to fully participate in quantifiable and productive economic activity contributes to their marginalisation in the informal economy. There has been little progress made in closing the gender gap in access to finance, despite decades of attention being paid to women as a significant client telle.

5 Challenges for Women's Financial Inclusion:-

Barred women are harder to identify. Household checks are precious and time consuming, but they're the only medium for relating people who are outside the banking system. Banks can survey their guests and study their deals, but this limits them to people who formerly have fiscal access.

Women are informationally underprivileged with lower and lower different networks, and are less likely to admit referrals from people within their networks. Women are more delicate to reach through the usual channels that target men, including pay envelope payments and remittance channels as well as savings accounts. In Eastern Europe and Central Asia, for illustration, only 18 percent of women report entering stipend into an account. Indeed with a scale up of digital pay envelope payments, only 29 percent of women report having entered stipend in the once time, compared with 49 percent of men. In South Asia, men are doubly as likely to have transferred domestic remittances within the once time and 6 percent more likely to have entered them. still, one channel in particular shows pledge. Findex data show that men and women have analogous rates of damage of government- to-person transfers. Providers have lower incitement to feed to women because the perimeters are lower and women bear further outspoken investment to bring on as guests.

How do you lower sale costs for someone who deals in small totalities? Women frequently prefer informal products, particularly for savings, and reaching them with formal products entails advanced costs in order to explain products to them and impact misters, musketeers, and other community leaders who women turn to for advice and protestation. Banks that successfully advanced to women possessed SME's frequently also givenon-financial services similar as leadership training. Social morals constrain women's demand for fiscal services. frequently times women aren't anticipated or encouraged to have fiscal independence. occasionally they've mobility constraints that make it delicate to engage with fiscal institutions. Women, Business and the Law counts 17 husbandry where misters can constrain their women mobility outside the home.

In worst case scripts, women act simply as a transfer medium for fiscal products to men, further distorting the nature of demand. A study by Natalia Rigol of Harvard University showed that women entrepreneurs frequently diverted finances meant for their own businesses to businesses run by the men in their homes. Women have lower access to technology, and with mobile phones being touted as the rearmost game changer that could radicalize rates of fiscal addition, the gender gap pitfalls adding if women aren't specifically targeted.

The GSMA estimates that 200 million smaller women than men enjoy a mobile phone across low and middle income countries. In India, where the government is enhancing sweats to promote digital finance, a woman is 36 percent less likely to enjoy a mobile phone than a man. The significance of women's access to finance goes beyond fiscal addition. Cuberes and Teignier estimate that in the Middle East and North Africa, the average income loss due to gender gaps in entrepreneurship and employment is 38 percent. Income losses in South Asia are estimated at 25 percent and at17.3 percent in Latin America and the Caribbean. As an enabler of education, employment and entrepreneurship, fiscal addition underpins statistics on issues similar as income.

By the Numbers:-

1. Just 72% of males and 65% of women, respectively, have bank accounts.

2. Less women than males own smartphones, which are essential for using digital banking services.

3. CFI conducted 30% more financial competence interviews with thought leaders and donors, financial service providers, financial inclusion and women's economic empowerment programmes.

4. Women make up 56% of the almost two billion people who are denied access to financial services globally.

Synopsis In order to study how processes of exclusion and constrained and unfavourable inclusion influence various women's labour market opportunities and outcomes in Lucknow, India, this research conducts comparative analyses across women's employment-status categories. It investigates whether, and under what circumstances, women's labour helps to reduce family poverty, as well as whether job kinds pay well and provide women in the home more say, one aspect of the empowering process. It concludes that social norms and obligations for reproductive work might result in constricted inclusion in the labour market, adversely influencing women's terms of incorporation, and that women's labour force involvement has a negligible impact on household and individual level development

results

Suggestions for Include Women in Finance by experts :-

The following suggestions are made in this brief to extend women's financial inclusion beyond having access to bank accounts:-

1. Recruit more women Business journalists. Business Correspondents (BCs) are retail representatives who offer banking services at customers' doorsteps in rural areas. Since its introduction in 2006, BCs have become the country's dominant method of delivering financial services. Women prefer going to a female BC because they find them more approachable and reliable. Less than 10% of BCs as of March 2022 are female. The mobility and literacy barriers that women encounter are avoided by the BC model.

2. Encourage women's use of and literacy in regard to digital tools. The inability to make transactions is a fundamental barrier preventing women from using formal financial services. Because they are less likely to acquire a phone, women are less likely to master digital financial skills. The 2014 National Digital Literacy Mission, one policy effort on digital literacy and skilling, shows how the corporate sector and CSOs can collaborate with the government in fostering digital literacy.

3. Consolidate confluence with tone- help groups. In India, tone-help groups(SHGs) have historically played an important part in the fiscal addition of women through the SHG- Bank relation Programme. The Bank Sakhis programme by the National Rural Livelihoods Mission trains SHG members to work as BCs in the pastoral sections. The programme has bettered women's exposure to fiscal services, in turn driving up deals in pastoral India. SHGs can also be tapped to run fiscal knowledge centres for women. Livelihood and skill-development programmes by SHGs can be integrated with other enterprise in digital fiscal addition.

4. Collect gender- disaggregated data and develop strategies to form women- centric approaches. India is a member of the Alliance for Financial Addition(AFI), a policy leadership alliance led by central banks and fiscal nonsupervisory institutions. As similar, it has pledged to close the gender gap in fiscal addition by enforcing the Denarau Action Plan espoused in 2016 by members of the AFI. One of the commitments under the Plan is to promote stylish practices in collecting, analysing, and using coitus- disaggregated data to promote fiscal addition for women. India can take this up as a policy ideal. Promote digital credit for medium and small businesses. India has anywhere

from13.5 to15.7 million women- possessed enterprises, up to 95 percent of which aremicro-businesses.

5.   Women- run businesses in India face a huge credit gap due to social impulses on the part of fiscal institutions on assessing their creditworthiness likewise, due to limited access to means and property, women face difficulty in carrying collateral. Fintech can play a part in bias-free digital lending to women-led enterprises. This can bring in formalisation and make women's donation to the frugality more visible.

Recommendations for development:

1. Legislative protections are required for ownership in the family's female head of household (as earlier ration cards under PDS were made in the name of the female head of the family).
2. Women are not subject to any restrictions or constraints when fulfilling Know Your Customer (KYC) procedures at banks.
3. No societal rules that discriminate against women in banks (friendly environment such as a bank sakhee appointed in Uttar Pradesh for SHGs under SRLM).
4. Opening and operating extension and outreach services—small retail locations of nationalised banks in rural areas—should be done by women.
5. Women have unrestricted access to the official labour market.
6. requiring women to receive financial literacy training.
7. Increased female participation in the financial sector (via reservation).
8. Create digital goods and services to help women.

THE ROLE OF NATIONAL LEGISLATIONS IN FACILITATING EFFECTIVE ONLINE DISPUTE RESOLUTION SYSTEM

Authored by:- T. Tahira Mehreen

V year BBA.,LL.B

ABSTRACT

ODR is critical in today's digital environment because it coincides with individuals' and organisations' changing requirements and expectations. It provides efficient, accessible, and cost-effective conflict resolution procedures, making it an essential component of modern justice systems and trade. As technology advances, ODR's role in fostering justice and efficiency in conflict resolution will only grow in importance. Because of its accessibility, convenience, cost-effectiveness,technology integration, worldwide reach, reduced case backlogs, environmental impact, and innovation, online dispute resolution (ODR) is critical in the digital era.

Individuals and corporations can engage in dispute resolution procedures from anywhere with ODR, removing the need for physical presence, travel, and scheduling difficulties. It also allows for real-time communication and document sharing, allowing it to be completed faster than traditional litigation. To improve the quality of dispute resolution, ODR platforms make use of innovative technology such as AI, machine learning, and secure communication protocols. ODR crosses jurisdictional lines, promoting global trade and lowering case backlogs. It also eliminates the need for physical travel and documentation, which contributes to a lower carbon impact. ODR platforms prioritise the user experience and promote innovation.

Online Dispute Resolution (ODR) is a method of resolving disputes using digital technology and the internet as the primary medium. It provides an alternative to traditional face-to-face or courtroom-based dispute resolution processes, encompassing tools and platforms designed to facilitate negotiations, mediation, arbitration, and adjudication online.

Keywords: ODR- Online Dispute Resolution, Arbitration and conciliation, Information Technology, Contract, Proceedings, Electronic Evidence , Judicial Precedents , Digital personal Data protection, Confidentiality, Security, dispute resolution. UNICTRAL.

DEVELOPMENT OF ODR:

ODR's evolution can be traced back to the late 20th century, with early experiments in the 1990s focusing on email and early web technologies for negotiation and mediation.

In the early 2000s, several countries and international organizations began exploring ODR solutions for e-commerce and consumer disputes. The United Nations Commission on International Trade Law (UNCITRAL) established the Working Group on ODR, emphasizing its importance for cross-border transactions.

In the mid-2000s, dedicated ODR platforms and services were developed, offering secure and structured online environments for parties to resolve disputes. Legal recognition in the 2010s and 2020s saw ODR gain legal recognition and support in various jurisdictions. With advancements in technology, ODR has become more sophisticated, with AI, machine learning, and blockchain technology being integrated into platforms. ODR's potential to transform dispute resolution in the digital age is significant, combining principles of fairness, accessibility, and efficiency.

INTRODUCTION:

ODR Players are those entities who offer online platforms to solve disputes between the aggrieved parties. ODR is the use of technology for resolving of disputes.

The proliferation of internet brought together people from different locations and jurisdictions to engage in virtual business transactions. This ultimately resulted in the emergence of numerous cross-border disputes, and as a result, creative methods of settling them were created by private organisations. The groundwork appears to be in place for ODR to become one of the primary dispute settlement methods in India, in part because to the urgency created by COVID-19.

The first such was eBay back in 1999. A customer could submit a complaint online and start a settlement procedure using the eBay platform. If the agreement couldn't be reached, an online mediation process would start. The platform's goal was to identify the issue and carry out automatic negotiation before mediating or arbitrating the dispute.

This paradigm, which has since developed into more sophisticated variations and is widely employed by both states and other private organisations, is known as ODR.

The United Nations Commission on International Trade Law ODR Working Group defines **ODR as "a mechanism for resolving disputes facilitated through the use of electronic communications and other information and communication technology".** In essence, ODR is simply e-ADR where interactions take place online using technology. Technology has been touted as being the "fourth party" in ODR.

ODR began and developed in the world of private, multinational organisations that provide online dispute resolution to parties, such as Smart settle, Cyber settle, and the Mediation Room.

The launch of "SUVAS" (Supreme Court Vidhik Anuvaad Software), a translation engine powered by artificial intelligence that converts court rulings from English to Indian languages. It provides multilingual in 9 Indian languages, now proposal has been made to involve 22 languages. This makes more accessible to the parties to use any documents in their own languages.

Recently, NITI Aayog hosted a meeting on "Catalysing Online Dispute Resolution in India" at which it brought together key stakeholders to work cooperatively to ensure measures are done to scale online dispute resolution in India. The discussion was organised in cooperation with Agami and Omidyar Network India.

It was acknowledged throughout the discussion that ODR has enormous potential for India, especially for small and medium-sized conflicts. It can improve access to justice and convenience of doing business because effective dispute resolution will be essential for overcoming the COVID-19's economic issues.

Courts Contribution in recognising ODR Mechanism

1. Video-conferencing as a mode for talking is recognized

The Supreme Court was crucial in laying the groundwork for the introduction of ODR in the nation. In **the State of Maharashtra v. Praful Desai case**, it recognised the viability of video conferencing as a method for gathering evidence and witness testimony and said that "virtual reality is the actual reality."

In **Grid Corporation of Orissa Ltd. v. AES Corporation**, the court decided that it was not required for people to sit next to each other in the same physical area if consultation could be accomplished using electronic media and remote conferencing. This decision continued a similar trend.

2. Electronic summons is recognised.

In **Central Electricity Regulatory Commission vs. National Hydroelectric Power Corporation Ltd**, Supreme Court approved serving of summons via. Email as well as other methods.

3. Validating online arbitration and agreement

Further, the court has recognised the validity of online arbitration in **Shakti Bhog v Kola Shipping and Trimex International v Vedanta Aluminium Ltd.** In both these cases the court has held that an online arbitration agreement is valid as long as it is compliant with **Section 4 and 5 of the Information Technology Act ("IT Act"), 2008 read with Section 65B of the Indian Evidence Act, 1872** and provisions of the Arbitration and Conciliation Act, 1996.

4. Evidence Admissibility of Electronic Records

Electronic evidence is admissible under Sec.65B of the Indian Evidence Act, 1872. In recent Years, the Supreme Court has improved this method for admissibility of electronic records by Judicial Precedents.

The Supreme Court has ruled that electronic evidence can be included as secondary evidence in cases, regardless of conformity with Sec.65B. This was overturned in 2014 in **Anwar P.V. vs. P.K Basheer**. In this case court ruled that "Section 65B is itself a complete code and that the requirements laid down must be followed while submitting any electronic record for inspection to court."

The court strengthened the procedure for electronic evidence admission in **M/s Meters and instruments Pvt. Ltd vs. Kanchan Mehta.** The court also suggested that minor disputes could be resolved online, such as traffic challans and cheque bouncing.

The current regulations contain measures that have made it possible to accommodate online operations, particularly the sharing of virtual papers and virtual hearings.

 Similarly, **the IT Act accords recognition to digital** signatures under **Section 4, 5, 10-A and 11-15** to provide validity to online contracts. This has been made possible by **adopting the UNCITRAL Model Law on Electronic Commerce in 1996 and the Model Law on Electronic Signatures in 2001**. This framework can continue to be the bedrock to ensure enforceability of ODR in the short run. In the long run however, specific recognition for ODR in all forms of dispute resolution – private and court-annexed ADR, would be ideal.

A few years ago the Department of Justice had published a list of institutions that have the capacity to resolve disputes online.

ADR's success is largely due to its confidentially component. There is obviously considerable cause for concern when this process is carried out online concerns data privacy both during and after proceedings. Ensuring that there exist norms and standards that require document encryption is one way to protect parties' interests.

Parliamentary Standing Committee Report (Virtual Courts) The government and judiciary have recently adopted technological assistance in the delivery of justice as a result of the COVID-19 pandemic's limitations. Technology has played a key role in helping court processes in recent months. The Department Related Parliamentary Standing Committee on Personnel, Public Grievances, Law and Justice recognised this impact of technology in its recent report on 'Functioning of the virtual courts/court procedures utilising video conferencing. "Report of the Expert Committee on Amendments to IT Act 2000

Legal Framework Facilitating ODR

- **Code of Civil Procedure, 1908- Section 89 of the CPC**, 1908 encourages disputants to utilise alternative dispute settlement methods. The court has the authority under Order X Rule 1A119 to order the parties to settle their issues through any alternative dispute resolution means. This is where ODR fits in.
- **Indian Evidence Act, 1872 - Sections 65-A and 65-B of** the Indian Evidence Act, 1872, provide requirements for admission and recognise electronic evidence. These provisions may serve as guidelines for exchanging virtual records and papers, as well as as conducting virtual hearings.

Section 65A & Section 65B are critical in aiding the admissibility and dependability of electronic evidence generated during ODR processes. They lay the legal groundwork for the use of electronic documents in dispute resolution and boost the general legitimacy of India's ODR platforms.

Admissibility of Electronic Evidence (Section 65A): Section 65A clarifies that electronic documents can be entered as evidence in judicial proceedings. This includes data, emails, digital documents, and any other electronic information.

Impact on ODR: Electronic records and communication are heavily used in ODR systems. Section 65A makes electronic evidence collected during ODR processes admissible in court, increasing the enforcement of ODR outcomes.

Certification of Electronic Evidence (Section 65B): Section 65B specifies the conditions for electronic evidence admissibility. It states that electronic records must be supported by a certificate certifying their accuracy and integrity.

Section 65B of the ODR platform ensures admissible electronic records of dispute-related communications and documents, enhancing trust and authenticity. It also promotes data integrity, preventing tampering or manipulation, and enhances the credibility of the ODR process by ensuring data integrity.

Section 65B allows **cross-examination** of the person who produced and issued the electronic evidence, impacting Online Dispute Resolution (ODR) proceedings. This reinforces the legal framework for ODR platforms in India, requiring providers to comply with Sections 65A and 65B to maintain the admissibility of electronic evidence in legal proceedings.

- ## Arbitration and Conciliation Act, 1996

The agreement, procedure, and ultimate award or settlement are the main provisions or processes of a dispute resolution process. The provisions of arbitration would be applicable because, similar to ODR, arbitration and mediation are frequently used as a tool to resolve disputes electronically. The following laws are recognised by the Arbitration and Conciliation Act and may also be used in the ODR procedure:

1. Arbitration Agreements:

Section 7(4)(b) of the 1996 Act, states that an arbitration agreement can be derived from exchange of letters, telex, telegram or other means of communication, including through electronic means. The 2015 Amendment Act inserted the words "including communication through electronic means" in Section 7(4)(b).

Trimex International Fze Limited, Dubai v. Vedanta Aluminium Ltd("Trimex case"), in which the Hon'ble Court stated that for a contract (whether electronic or otherwise) to be valid, it must satisfy the requirements of Section 10 of the Indian Contract Act, 1872, recognised a contract that was executed through the exchange of e-mails. The same holds true for an arbitration agreement. The Hon'ble Supreme Court concluded in **Vidya Drolia v. Durga Trading Corpn,** that the fulfilment of legal conditions under the Indian Contract Act and Arbitration and Conciliation Act is necessary for an arbitration agreement to be effective. The Apex Court additionally acknowledged the validity of the arbitration clause in the Trimex case if the contract was signed via email correspondence. The court ruled that even in the absence of a written contract between the parties, it would be feasible to draw inferences of a signed contract from a variety of documents that were sent between them in the form of letters, telegrams, telex messages, and other forms of electronic communication that were duly approved and signed by all parties.

The Apex Court gave Section 7 of the Arbitration Act a purposeful reading in the case of **Shakti Bhog Foods Limited v. Kola Shipping Limited** and decided that an inference must be made from the exchange of emails, letters, or faxes even if the agreement was not signed by the parties. Based on the rulings in the Trimex and Shakti Bhog instances, it can be concluded that an electronic arbitration agreement is legitimate and enforceable if it complies with the requirements of the Arbitration Act.

2.   Arbitration Proceedings:

Arbitral proceedings are fundamental in nature and should be clearly outlined in agreements or institutional rules. Parties can send statements of claim and defense electronically, emails, or couriers.

The Arbitration and Conciliation Act, 1996 aims to provide quick and effective remedies to disputes through Online Arbitration. Technical difficulties, such as electricity or system failures, must be addressed in the agreement or institutional rules to ensure the system's functionality.

The International Chamber of Commerce (ICC) has framed standards for Online Arbitration, including file names, originator identification, document class, arbitration place, email transmission mode, attachment format, and audio and video conferencing rules. Parties must decide on procedural requirements for virtual proceedings, including exchange of pleadings, video conferencing, and audio conferencing.

In cases where parties and arbitrators are placed at different ends of the system, allegations of non-compliance of Section 12 and Section 18 of the Act may arise. Therefore, rules for holding virtual proceedings should ensure equality and impartiality for parties.

3. Arbitral Award- Section 31 read with Section 5 & 15 of Information Technology Act,200

Section 31 of A&C Act, 1996 deals with the form and effect of arbitral award. It specifies that award must be made in writing and signed by the arbitrator(s). ection 31 of the Arbitration and Conciliation Act addresses the form and impact of arbitral awards, requiring the arbitrator to make and sign the award in writing and present it electronically. This allows for efficient enforcement of arbitral awards in ODR processes, which often result in settlements.

Section 15 of the IT Act and Section 31 of the Arbitration and Conciliation Act recognize the evidentiary value of electronic records, which are used as evidence in ODR platforms during dispute settlement. This ensures that arbitral awards and settlements made by ODR are legally valid and enforceable, benefiting ODR participants.

Section 5 of the Information Technology Act, 2000 provides that the digital signature have the same effect as a paper signature.

- **<u>Information Technology Act, 2000</u>**
  1. **Section 4 of IT Act, 2000- Legal recognition of electronic records.**

In cases where a law specifies that information or another matter must be in writing, typewritten, or printed form, that requirement is still considered to have been met if the information or other matter is:

(a) rendered or made available in an electronic form, and

(b) accessible enough to be used for a future reference.

Section 4 confirms that electronic record hold legal validity, making them admissible as evidence in ODR proceedings.

2. **Section 5 of IT Act, 2000- Legal recognition of [electronic signature]. –**

In cases where a law stipulates that a person's signature must be affixed to a document or that information must be authenticated in this way, the requirement will be deemed satisfied—regardless of any other provisions in the law—if the information or matter is authenticated using an electronic signature that is attached in accordance with any rules the Central Government may have established.

For the purposes of this section, "signed," along with its grammatical derivatives and related expressions, shall, with relation to a person, mean affixing of his handwritten signature or any mark on any document, and the term "signature" shall be interpreted in accordance with that definition.

ODR platforms handle sensitive data, and the use of digital signature is essential for verifying the identity of parties and maintaining data security, it ensures trustworthiness of ODR processes.

Public-key cryptography is a technique for authentication that is used in digital signatures. In order to increase trust, it is crucial to ensure the validity, integrity, and non-repudiation of data communication.

The 2000 Information Technology Act Sections 4 and 5, recognise electronic records and electronic signatures. A requirement for the complete digitization of justice delivery processes may be this legal recognition.

3. **Validity of contracts formed through electronic means. –**

When proposals are communicated, accepted, or revoked as part of the formation of a contract using electronic means, such a contract shall not be deemed to be unenforceable solely on the basis that such electronic forms or means were employed for that purpose.

The validity of contracts executed through electronic means is a foundational element of ODR. ODR platforms must operate within legal framework established for electronic contracts, digital signatures, data security and privacy. This section recognises the contract in electronic mode and thus is enforceable in ODR.

- **Digital personal data protection Act,2023 [DPDP]- Data Security and Confidentiality:**

The data protection act primarily focuses on data protection and privacy rights. The DPDP has relevance to ODR platforms. The provisions of the DPDP Bill have a direct and applicable impact on ODR platforms." Because ODR systems gather, process, and store personal data in the course of dispute resolution, they fall under the purview of the DPDP Bill.

To preserve individuals' privacy rights and conform to the legal framework governing the handling of personal data in the digital era, ODR providers must ensure complete compliance with the data protection obligations stated in the DPDP Bill."

This emphasises that ODR platforms process personal data, they are subject to the DPDP Bill's laws, making compliance with the bill's provisions a critical component of their operations.

Conclusion

National legislation is critical in shaping and supporting effective ODR systems. Legislation helps promote trust in online dispute resolution by providing a legal framework that handles issues such as data protection, consumer rights, enforcement, and cybersecurity. It also ensures that it corresponds with the legal norms and standards of a given jurisdiction. As ODR evolves, legislation will change to meet the needs of modern dispute resolution in the digital age. The aforementioned laws are among those that govern ODR platforms and give participants confidence that they can engage in an efficient dispute resolution process, which supports an efficient remedy as well.

In **Grid Corporation of Orissa Ltd. vs. AES Corporation** the Supreme Court explicitly mentions that : "when an effective consultation can be achieved by resort to electronic media and remote conferencing, it is not necessary that the two persons required to act in consultation with each other must necessarily sit together at one place unless it is the requirement of law or of the ruling contract between the parties".

The judgement emphasis the importance of ODR in digital age which offers several advantages such as Efficiency and cost-effectiveness, accessibility, time-effective, confidentiality, speedy resolution. Online dispute resolution (ODR) is increasingly popular in India compared to traditional legal systems. However, many people are unaware of ODR and rely on traditional legal systems. In comparison to Western countries, many companies lack online dispute resolution facilities. Strengthening ODR can reduce the burden on traditional legal systems and improve dispute resolution efficiency. India currently has over 450,000 pending consumer cases in 630 courts, with 40% related to defective products and banking, and 60% related to insurance, housing, and medical negligence cases.

WHAT IS UNIFORM CIVIL CODE ? :
 NEED AND SIGNIFICANCE

Authored by:- SHARVI PANDEY

There is nothing non-secular or sectarian in demanding that the provisions of Indian civil laws should apply evenhandedly to all said by Amartya Sen.

Recently, a bill was presented in the Rajya Sabha for the creation of a commission drafting Uniform Civil Code. The bill was submitted by BJP member Kirodi Lal Meena with the aim of creating a national inspection and investigation commission to create a UCC. It was opposed by the oppossition members of Trinamool Congress (TMC), Marumalarchi Dravida Munnetra Kazhagam (MDMK), Rashtriya Janata Dadl (RJD), Samajwadi Party (SP), Communist Party of India (CPI), CPI (Marxist), Nationalist Congress Party (NCP), and Congress on the grounds of infringement of the rights of minority, violation of Article 25 of the Constitution which gives religious freedoms to citizens and permits religious organizations to carry their own affairs. Much debate has been surrounding in the recent times.

The idea behind a UCC is to have commom legal framework that governs subjetcs like marriage, inheritance, succession etc because right now, in India these matters are governed by diferent personal laws which leads to confusion, discrimination and injustice.

What is UCC?

UCC or Uniform Civil Code means that there should be a common civil code for all the citizens of the country, irrespective of their religion. And it should be applicable on all the citizens uniformly. It should cover areas like – marriage, inheritance, divorce, succession, adoption.

Article 44 of the Constitution in the Directive Principles of State Policy states that " State should endeavour to secure a uniform civil code for all it's citizens throughout the territory of India." However, according to the Article 37 of the Constitution, DPSPs are not enforceable in the court of law unlike fundamental rights.

Historical Background

Pre-Independence
The Lex Loci Report of October 1840, stressed on the importance and necessity of uniformity in the codification of Indian law, relating to crimes, evidence and contract. But, it also recommended that personal laws of Hindus and Muslims should be kept outside such codification.

The Queen's 1859 Proclamation- It promised absolute non-interference in religious matters.

So while criminal laws were codified and became common for the whole country, personal laws continue to be governed by separate codes for different communities.

Post-Colonial era (1947-1985)

During the drafting of the constitutions, some of the leaders like Jawharlal Nehru and Dr. B.R. Ambedkar were in favour of UCC. Dr. B.R. Ambekar belived that UCC is crucial for ensuring national integration, gender equality and secularism. However, some of the members of the constituent assembly were against it, claiming that they should not tamper with the religious laws.

So, instead UCC was included in the Directive Principles of State Policy in Article 44 due to oppostion by some of the constituent assembly memebers due to lack of awareness.

Constitutional reforms related to UCC

1. The Hindu Code Bill

The main objective of the Hindu Code Bill was to form a common civic code that would replace Hindu personal law which was amended to a certain extent by the Britishers. So, the government of the former Prime Minister Jawaharlal Nehru introduced the Hindu Code Bill in which women's rights were promoted and gender equaltiy was ensured. But this bill faced severe opposition. So, it's diluted version was passed, which consisted of four different laws namely,

Hindu Marriage Act, 1955
Hindu Succession Act, 1956
Hindu Minority and Guardianship Act, 1956
Hindu Adoption and Maintenance Act, 1956

1. Shah Bano Case

In the case of **Mohd. Ahmad Khan v/s Shah Bano Begum - (Air 1985 Scr (3) 844),** a 73 years old women, filed a suit of maintenance against her husband, Ahmad Khan, who had divorced by using Triple Talaq. The Supreme court ruled in her favour and asked her husband to pay her maintenance under Section 125 of the CrPC which applied to all citizens, provided for maintenance of the wife.

Impact after the ruling:

Country wide protests were held by the Muslim Community as the ruling was against the Muslim Personal Laws, according to which, the Muslim women were entitled to a maintenance for Iddat period(for 90 days after the divorce). So, under pressure, the government passed The Muslim Women's (Right to protection on divorce) Act (MWA) in 1986,which made Section 125 inapplicable on Muslim women.

1. Sarla Mudgal Case

In the case of **SARLA MUDGAL v. UNION OF INDIA AIR 1995 SC 1531**, the question was whether a Hindu husband married under the Hindu Marriage Act solemnize a second marriage after embracing Islam. The Court held that a Hindu marriage can only be dissolved under the Hindu Marriage Act. And if a person, after converting to Islam, solemnizes a second marriage without the dissolving the first one, it would be considered an offence under the

Section 494 of IPC.

The court observed that Muslim personal law permits bigamy which is inconsistent with the other communites' personal laws and is also immoral. Therefore, there is need for a common civil code that will remove the loopholes of personal laws and promote gender equality.

1. **Daniel Latifi Case**

In the case of **Danial Latifi & Anr vs Union Of India, 28 September 2001,** the Muslim Women's (Right to protection on divorce) Act, 1986 was challenges on the grounds that law was discriminatory and it violates the right to equality of Muslim women provided under Article 14 of the Constitution as against the women of other communities who are provided maintenance for life under the section 125 of Crpc while according to the Muslim personal law it is the duty of the husband to provide maintenance to the wife only for the Iddat period. Also, there is a violation of Article 21 as the law would leave Muslim women destitute. The Court held that the MWRPD Act, 1986 was valid as the husband has to provide the maintenance for the Iddat period after contemplating all the future needs of the wife and making preparations in advance, thereby striking a balance between MWRPD Act, 1986 and Crpc.

Countries following UCC

There are many countries all over the world that follow Uniform Civil Code such as Pakistan, Bangladesh, Malaysia, Turkey, Indonesia, Sudan, Egypt, America, Ireland, etc. There is a common civil code for all the citizens and there are no separate personal laws for different religions.

Why do we need a Uniform Civil Code?

1. **National Integration** – As we know that India is diverse country with people of different religions, caste, creed. So, it will help in clubbing all the people under one common civil code,no matter which religion, tribe or community they are from. It will reaffirm the notion of **"one nation, one law"**, which will also promote the idea of Unity in diversity.

1. **Promotion of gender equality** – Many personal laws in India have discriminatory provisions for women relating to the matters of divorce, Inheritance or marriage. For example, the Muslim Personal law permits bigamy which is against the public morals and discriminatory against women. So, after the implementation of UCC these loopholes in the personal laws can be eradicated and promote equality and justice.

1. **Example of Goa's Civil Code** – Many supporters of UCC cite the example of Goa as it has been following **The Portuguese Civil Code, 1867**, a form of Uniform Civil Code. It is a set of laws that governs all the people of Goa irrespective of their religion. And it has been successfully implemented in Goa. So, this sets a strong precedent.

1. **Promoting Secularism** – If UCC is implemented, it doesn't mean the religious freedom of people will be curtailed. Instead it will only eradicate the age old discriminatory and unjust practices in various personal laws of all religions and will make sure that everyone is treated

equally irrespective of their religion.

1. **<u>Help in reducing vote bank politics</u>** – There have been many occasions in the past when the bill for implementing Uniform Civil Code has been introduced in the Parliament and it could not proceed further due to strong opposition from the political parties because it will hurt the sentiments of religious fundamentalists which would result in a reduction of vote share in the elections for the parties.

So, it will help in reducing the vote bank politics that every political party indulges in the elections.

<u>Arguments against Uniform Civil Code</u>

1. **<u>Imposition of Hinduised code</u>** – Some minorities have misconceptions that UCC would be molded according to Hindu rituals and traditions. It is believed that majority views would be imposed on them. For example, if UCC makes provisions for family disputes over property, then those legal provisions would also be imposed on other religions.

1. **<u>Curtailment of religious freedom</u>** – The main argument is that implementation of UCC will lead to violation of the freedom to profess and practice any religion. For example, Article 25-28 give religious freedom to citizens and allow the religious communities to conduct their own affairs. Also, Article 29 gives them the right to conserve their culture.

1. **<u>Threat to cultural diversity</u>** – India is famous for it's rich culture and heritage. Different religious communities have their own culture and traditions. However if UCC will implemented, then it will lead to a homogenization of laws, because of which cultural diversity will be lost. Also, it is violation of Article 29 which gives them the right to conserve their culture.
1. Protection of Minority Rights: One of the main concerns is the impact on minority communities because Personal laws are deeply intertwined with the religious identity and practices of these communities. Imposing a common civil code may dilute the unique rights and protections enjoyed by minority groups. It could also erode their cultural autonomy. Protecting minority rights and preserving their distinct practices is crucial for a democracy.

<u>Suggestions for implementation of UCC</u>

First of all, People should be aware of the loopholes in the personal laws and the need to reform them. This should be initiated by the communities themselves. Only when and if the rights are violated, legal intervention must be made.

Secondly, the transformation should be gradual. Government must take a piecemeal approach and implement implement one single reform at a time.

Third, There should be consultations with the stakeholders. Like, the **22nd Law Commission** has sought the views of religious organisations and general public for UCC. So, thorough investigations, discussions and consultations should be take place to avoid any ambiguities

The Way Forward for UCC: Gradual Change

Uniform Civil Code will definitely be a revolutionary change in the history of our country which a unique blend of different religions, tribes, communities each having their own set of age old codified laws. There are differences of opinions among different stakeholders, especially religious communities. And as we know it is easy to perpetuate communal disharmony in India. And our political leaders in order to gain vote bank would be ready to sacrifice communal harmony. Keeping in mind, our harsh realities - the Gujarat riots, post- independence bloodshed, as of now, UCC cannot be implemented without bloodshed. So, a consensus should be made gradually. Political leaders should keep their political gains aside and promote the need for a Uniform Civil Code among the general public. Serious discussions about it's pros and cons should held with the stakeholders. And there should a consensus made to implement the Uniform Civil Code for the entire republic of India

SAME-SEX MARRIAGE:

A Social- Legal Analysis

Authored By- ANUJ PRATAP SINGH[1] and ARVIND KUMAR[2]

"Race, gender, religion, sexuality, we are all people and that's it. We're all people. We're all equal." -Connor Franta**Abstract**

The sanctioning of same sex marriage has been a fight that has been seething since theold time. Historians frequently reference back to the precolonial times while talkingabout same-sex love and its pervasiveness in mythology, vernacular literature andreligious text. However, many go against homosexuality in light of the thinking that it buys into western propensities. It took many years of appeals and judgments for thedraconian colonial-era hostile to homosexuality regulation to be switched in India. But when, there will be probability to legitimate same-sex marriage? Bynot permitting same sexual, state is making victimization same sex couples and against same sex marriage with a conviction that marriage is the establishment for procreation, same-sex couple without the capacity to have their own youngster, ought not bepermitted the right of marriage.

Socio-strict opinions, eccentric hypothesis, basic freedoms, and established ethical quality are completely discussed and inspected to presume that not exclusively is thelawful acknowledgment of same-sex relationships critical for the progressionof LGBTQIA+(*Lesbian, Gay, Bisexual ,Transgender, Queer or Questioning, Intersex, Asexual, and more*), yet in addition an assistance to partake in the crucial privileges of sexual minorities. Furthermore, in this paper we will expose the 'westernphilosophy contention, countering through artistic and realistic proof of homosexuality apparent across India's landmarks and sacred writings and furthermorediscusses the penetration of pilgrim ethics and how the English man's and their particular strict rules dirtied the implication of same-sex love in India. This paper examines the significance of lawful acknowledgment of same-sex marriages in India. **Keywords:** *LGBTQIA+, Homosexuality, Constitution, Same-Sex marriage.*

[1] Author is an B.A.LL.B 3

[rd]year student at Maharishi Law School, Maharishi University of Information Technology, Noida, India.

[2] Author is an Mechanical Engineering Graduate from Faculty Of Engineering And Technology, University of Lucknow, Lucknow(U.P), India.

I. INTRODUCTION

From the ancient time society used to accept that there are just two orientationcommunities that exist in the world yet they some the way in which they neglected, denied and would not acknowledge the presence of different communities likehomosexuality or realized by other name like same sex love, transsexual, third gender and in now days we articulate them as LGBTQIA+

LGBTQIA+ today isn't simply a word however a trepidation, a no and an infectionthat spreads by seeing, knowing and perceiving, assuming that an everyday personstays with individuals of this community, he also will become like them. All along, individuals have had a specific mentality that nature has made just twosexes, male and female.

Aside from these, anything that different sexes are against nature, as indicatedbyindividuals, love relations must be between a man and a women and are like marriage. Since old times, the general public has given significance to the marriage of manandwomen and has given them lawful acknowledgment.

The third gender community known as LGBTQIA+ has battled fromhere onward, indefinitely seemingly forever to get equivalent regard, equivalent security, equivalent regulation and valuable potential for success to get having and position, to gainappreciation in the general public.

Many fights and mobilizes have been finished by them, a considerable lot of themwork and some don't and presently numerous regulations have been made for themselves and numerous changes have been made to serve that community yet not ready to checked and sanctioned there marriage yet.

Sanctioning LGBTQIA+ marriage is the greatest issue and battle for this communitythe supreme court of India allowed the homo couple to remain in live-in-relationshipas by struck down the *Section 377 of Indian Penal Code* however not allowed themthe right of marriage. The public authority and government of India is ceaselesslycontradicting the idea of same sex marriage by saying that this will upset the Indian
culture and illegal of nature according to the general public the marriage is ceremonybetween a men and a women.
Individuals in India restricting the LGBTQIA+ people group for quite a while bythis isn't the piece of Indian culture and express it as an unfamiliar practice.

Lets view the notable foundation and background of homosexuality in India;

A. ANCIENT INDIA:

Many Religious Text, Verses, Books, Vedas, Puranas, and scriptures and been foundthat depict the figure of our old India and gives the possibility of his flourishingandinformation about the Indian culture. And furthermore shows that the idea of homosexuality is a piece of Indian culture all along.

1. The story of Varuna and Mitra

Mitra-Varuna are alluded to in the ancient Indian sacred text of the Rigveda. Theyareboth viewed as Ādityas, or divinities associated with the Sun; and they are defenders who manage the widespread waters. They are portrayed riding a shark or crocodiletogether. At times they are depicted situated next to each other on a brilliant chariot drawn by seven swans.

Old Brahmana texts partner Mitra and Varuna with the two lunar stages and same-sexrelations. Bhagavata Purana (6.18.3) records Varuna and Mitra as having youngsters through non-vaginal sex. Agastya and Vasistha were brought into the world fromwater pots after Mitra and Varuna released their semen within the sight of Urvasi. This record is like Gay couples having youngsters through proxy moms in present daylike surrogacy.[3]

2. The story of King Bhagiratha

Ruler Dilip, a sovereign of the Suryavansh administration of Ramayana, was extremely disturbed that he had no child or replacement to proceed withhis inheritance. This was the genealogy where Lord Rama was conceived. He put forth

[3] Mitra and Varuna- The same-sex couple in Hindu mythology – GayIndia. [online]. Available at: https://gayrightsindia.wordpress.com/2016/10/28/mitra-and-varuna-the-same-sex-couple-in-hindu-mythology/..

endless attempts and did extreme retribution to get a child. This was hazardous reallyon the grounds that Ayodhya missing the mark on ruler, yet additionally profoundlyinlight of the fact that as per the enormous plan, Vishnu must be brought into the worldin a similar genealogy. The accidental stopping point of progression was unquestionably not uplifting news for the divine beings. At the point whenthestressed spouses moved toward their family priest for guidance, he guaranteed themthat a child would before long be brought into the world to them. He arrangedamixture for themselves and urged them to take part in sex - subsequently laying out acaring relationship. It's undeniably true that their relationship was not just in light of asexual result to save the realm, yet was the start of a genuine romance story betweenthe two co-spouses after the demise of their husbands. Not long after the sexual experience between the co-spouses started, the senior of the two, sovereign Mala, imagined and brought forth a child boy. Since the youngster was brought intotheworld from the association of two ladies, from two bhagas (female organs), he was named Bhagiratha.[4]

3. Sudyumna / Ila son of manu and sharaddha

It is said that every one of the administrations of people have begun fromManu. Manu stayed childless for quite a while after his union with Shraddha. He chose topetition the Divine beings for a child to sustain his bloodline. With the assistance of his master Sage Vashishtha he directed a fire penance in the distinction of twin Divinebeings Mitra and Varuna. They showed up and conceded his desire for a child. Ayoung lady Ila was brought into the world to Shraddha. Manu was not fulfilled, inlight of the fact that he had wanted a child. He requested that Vashishtha utilize his ability to transform the kid into a kid. Vashishtha transformed

Ila into Sudyumnaamale. In any case, fate had its own arrangements. Sudyumna was riding close toMount Sumeru during a hunting endeavor with his men. Following a deer theyentered a forest called Sukumara. The second his entourage arrived at the middle, theygenerally turned female, men, ruler and ponies.

[4] Tracing the legend of King Bhagiratha's Birth Out of Queer Romance. [online]. Available at: https://www.bonobology.com/tracing-the-legend-of-king-bhagirathas-birth/..

The woods was a confidential shower for Goddess Parvati. To monitor her security, Ruler Shiva had charmed the spot. Any male would go to female assuming he set his foot inside. Sudyumna sent for Sage Vashishtha, who attempted to conciliate Shiva toexcuse him and reestablish his manliness.

Shiva couldn't switch the impact of charms however he could change thema piece. He conceded that Sudyumna would on the other hand live as a female and male both. He would fail to remember all that he did in his substitute way of life as a lady whenhe transformed into a man. His memory would switch as well, to save himfromlivingwith culpability. Vashishtha acknowledged destiny. He left Ila in the woods. He knewonce he transformed into Sudyumna, he would get back.

Meandering in the forest Ila met planet Budh, the ill-conceived child of Chandra theMoon God and Tara. Budh was entirely educated and devout. He proposed to Ila andthey wedded. Their child Pururava was brought into the world to Ila. Since Pururavawas the grandson of Chandra, his relatives were known as Chandravanshis.

Albeit this story portrays the change of Sudyumna to Ila as complete actual change, it very well may be a metaphorical portrayal of his double sexual characters in a solitarybody - a sexually unbiased individual, who lived both as a man and a lady. Imagine a scenario in which Sudyumna had an issue of sexual separation (DSD)?what in the event that he had (5ARD). imagine a scenario where he had a genotype that was 46 XY as Vashishta planned initially. what's more, that he did have a femaleaggregate at a birth?
[5]

4. Hanuman in ramayana

In the Valmiki Ramayana, lord Rama's devotee and companion Hanuman is saidtohave seen Rakshasa ladies kissing and embracing other women. The lady were restingon each other with one lady heads on another bosoms, that lady lying on the thighs of another framing a festoon . The dresses of a portion of the ladies were not set up.[6]

5. Lord Ayyappa

[5] The curious case of Sudyumna: A tale of sex reversal from the Bhagavata Purana - PMC. [online]. Available at: https://www.ncbi.nlm.nih.gov/pmc/articles/PMC3712375/..

[6] Chapter 9–Hanuman enters the inner buildings of Ravana | Sundara Kandam.. Jai Ram. [online]. Available at: https://sundaragandam.wordpress.com/2012/06/17/chapter-9hanuman-enters-the-inner-buildings-of-ravana/..

Ayyappa = Ayya (Shiva) + Appa(Ruler Vishnu).

Ruler Ayyapan or likewise called as Ayyappa, is the Hindu God revered for the most part in the southern piece of India. He is known to be conceived out of the associationof master Shiva and Ruler Vishnu who was in his main female structure, Mohini. Ruler Vishnu then, at that point, shows up as Mohini and this leaves Master Shivahypnotized. He in a split second succumbs to her magnificence and conquers his energy.

This makes sense of his heavenly powers which are a blend of the powers of bothruler Shiva and Master Vishnu. The amazingly popular sanctuary in Kerala's Sabrimala needs no presentation. It is devoted to the love of Master Ayyappa whois additionally called Manikanta.[7]

6. Lord Rama in Ramayana

In the Sundar Kaand of the Ramayana, there is a story that has given the transsexual community in India its character. At the point when lord Rama was leaving for his 14-drawn out exile, every one of the animals, His adherents of the realmfollowed himtothe Forest to say goodbye to him. They were heartbroken to see their cherished princeleave and anxious to follow him till the end. However, when Lord Rama figuredout their goal, he asked each Nar, Nari, Pashu and Pakshi to get back. In any case, hedidn't specify the kinnars (transsexuals). As the kinnars say that We were neither Nar nor Nari. So we remained on in the forest, hanging tight for Ram's return.

At the point when Lord rama returned and found kinnars as yet hanging tight for him, he was so moved by their confidence that he favored them with the ability to bringbest of luck, and furthermore to revile. Indeed, even today, kinnars are welcome topromising events like weddings and labors, to bring best of luck.[8]

7. Shikandi in Mahabharata

[7] The Story of Ayyappa - TemplePurohit - Your Spiritual Destination | Bhakti, Shraddha Aur Ashirwad. [online]. Available at: https://www.templepurohit.com/the-story-of-ayyappa/..

[8] Reclaiming What Belongs To Them With Ram's Blessings. [online]. Available at: https://www.outlookindia.com/national/reclaiming-what-belongs-to-them-with-ram-s-blessings-magazine-226603..

In Mahabharata, subsequent to being kidnapped by Bhishma for his step siblinganddismissed by him in marriage, Princess Amba ended her life and committed to get her payback from Bhishma. Amba was reborn to Lord Drupada and named Shikhandini. At an eligible age, Shikhandini was hitched, to a princess. On the wedding night, inany case, the lady found that Shikhandi was a lady and she took off to her dad. Thedad of the bride of the hour who requested confirmation that Shikhandini was a man, and took steps to go after Lord Drupada's realm with a military assuming it was demonstrated in any case. Shikhandini embarrassed consequently, went tothetimberland to take her life yet was saved by a forest soul, Sthuna. Sthuna on learningof Shikhandini's aggravation - that Shikhandini was raised as a kid and felt and hadasimilar outlook as a man, however had a body that was of a lady - loanedhis masculinity to Shikhandini for one evening. Shikhandini could demonstrate that hewas a man and the new lady returned to her significant other. At the point whenShikhandini went to return his masculinity to the forest spirit, their chief was movedby his genuineness and permitted him to keep it until the end of time. As the storywent, she performed starknesses and changed her sex to become Shikhandi. Inthebattel of Kurukshetra, Bhishma remembered him as Shikandini, Amba renewed, andhe would have rather not battled with a "lady". On the 10th day of the conflict, Bhishma had to bring down his weapons as Shikhandi rode in Arjuna's chariot. Arjuna took cover behind Shikhandi and went after Bhishma with his arrows. Hence, Shikhandi was instrumental in Bhishma's passing in the Kurukshetra and the triumphof Pandavas. Hence, the Shikhandini became Shikhandi who was a man. Shikhandi was a trans manly strange character.[9]

B. MEDIEVAL INDIA :

A period where the new realms were laid out numerous invaders comes to India andgot radical changes Indian culture. Yet, we found many traces of existingof homosexuality in this era.

1. Alauiddin Khilji and Malif Kafur

Relatively few are know all about Alauddin Khilji's gay relationship with Malik Kafur.

[9] Trans masculinity in Indian Mythology: Misinterpreted, forgotten? | Heinrich Böll Stiftung | India Office. [online]. Available at: https://in.boell.org/en/2022/02/28/trans-masculinity-indian-mythology#_edn5..

Khilji's genuine name was Ali Gurshasp. He was both a nephew and child in-lawof Jalaluddin, who established the groundwork of the Khilji line in India in 1290subsequent to dismissing the Mamluks. Khilji turned into the legislative leader of few territories under the Delhi Sultanate. He declared himself theRuler of Delhi subsequent to killing his father by marriage and uncle Jalaluddinin1296 AD.Malik Kafur was a valiant clean shaven attractive eunuch. Alauddin Khilji had a soft spot for smooth young men. As per authentic sources, he had a fewthousand clean shaven young men in his group of concubines. He purchased Kafur for 1000 dinars during his Gujarat undertaking. Exploiting Khilji's shortcoming, Kafur surrendered and took total benefit to ascend to positions of influence, by effectivelyattacking realms, winning conflicts, ravaging riches and switching numerous over completely to Islam. Writer Ziauddin Barani, likewise a political mastermind of theDelhi Sultanate in the 14 hundred years, has referenced about the gay illicit relationship between Alauddin

Khilji and Malik Kafur in his book Tarikh-e FiruzShahi. Alauddin was so charmed by Malik Kafur that the Ruler generally gave himthe most elevated respect, contrasted with his different companions and assistants. According to accounts by Ziauddin Barani, when Alauddin was sick and was losinghis memory and his detects, he had fallen profoundly and frantically infatuated withMalik Kafur. He even endowed him with 'the obligation of the public authorityandthe control of the workers'. As per Ruth Vanita and Saleem Kidwai, bothgayexaminations researchers who concentrated on Barani's book, Khilji and Kafur werein a gay relationship.[10]

2. Babar and Baburi

Babur, an Islamic intruder of Turkic drop, is broadly prestigious as the organizer behind the blood-stained Mughal domain which is recorded to have mistreated local Indians under Islamic patriarchy.Babur was a self broadcasted bi-sexual, on the off chance that not gay, Islamic ruler. As per the Baburnama (the individual diaries of themain Mughal Head), a 17 year old Babur fell frantically enamored with a moreyouthful kid named 'Baburi' in Urdu Market. There is some disarray over the age of the kid, most trust him to be a teen despite the fact that there are the individuals who

[10] How Malik Kafur's Gay Mate Alauddin Khilji Was Wounded by Gora Singh. [online]. Available at: https://www.myindiamyglory.com/2018/07/05/how-malik-kafurs-gay-mate-alauddin-khilji-was-wounded-by-gora- singh/..

accept he was a pre-youngster.

"In those leisurely days I discovered in myself a strange inclination….. I ammaddened and aflicted myself for a boy in the camp-bazar, his very name, Baburi, fitting in. Up till then I had had no inclination for any-one,indeed of love and desire, either by hear-say or experience, I had not heard, I had not talked. Fromtime totimeBaburi used to come to my presence but out of modesty and bashfulness, I could never look straight at him; how then could I make conversation (ikhtildt) and recital (hikdyat)? In my joy and agitation I could not thank him (for coming); howwas it possible for me to reproach him with going away? What power had I to commandtheduty of service to myself?

One day, during that time of desire and passion when I was going with companions along a lane and suddenly met him face to face, I got into such a state of confusionthat I almost went right of . To look straight at him or to put words together was impossible. With a hundred torments and shames, I went on." (Ref: Baburnama, Vol. 1, pg 120)

As a matter of fact, Babur composes that he meandered wherever while profoundlypondering youthful Baburi's magnificence, and created a few couplets in Turki tolaudthe kid's clear comeliness.

So frantically infatuated was the Mughal ruler with the kid, he consistently composedcouplets portraying his affection for Baburi. For example,

Couplet 1- Out of myself desire rushed me, unknowing, That this is so with the lover of a fairy-face.

Couplet 2- Nor power to go was mine, nor power to stay; I was just what you mademe, o thief of my heart. (Source: Baburnama, Vol. 1, pg 121) It is said that Babur had numerous Eunuchs in the Mughal arrays of mistresses under him. The Mughal warriors normally took the ladies and young men of realms theyattacked and sent them to the collections of mistresses. The young men were typicallymutilated and transformed into eunuchs to give sexual fulfillment to the aristocrats. It is accepted that homosexuality was extremely normal in Muslim realms around then, and was genuinely normal for little fellows to be taken part in sexual exercises inarrays of mistresses show to the sovereigns.[11]

[11] Tales from the Baburnama: Babur and his love for a young boy. [online]. Available at: https://www.opindia.com/2020/09/tales-from-the-baburnama-babur-and-his-love-for-a-young-boy-homosexuality lgbt/..

3. Sufi Siant Bulleh Shah and Murshid Shah Inayat

The narrative of the connection between Bulleh Shah and Shah Inayat Qadiri inseventeenth Century Punjab.

Shah Inayat Qadiri was a Shaikh (profound educator) to numerous in the Punjabdistrict of present-day Pakistan. Shah Inayat came from an Arain (landscapers, vegetable-producers, viewed as a "lower") rank.

Bulleh Shah is famously known as Syed Abdullah Shah Qadri. He was a prestigious Sufi Holy person of India in the seventeenth century Promotion. He spreadthemessage of adoration and otherworldliness past the hindrances of rank, doctrine andreligion. Bulleh Shah was brought into the world around 1680 Promotion in UchhGalaniyan. His, father Shah Muhammad Dervesh, was an educated individual, whohad procured great information on Arabic and Persian dialects and a decent comprehension of the Blessed Quran.

Bulleh Shah, an Ashraf Syedi (considered "upper" rank), was searching for suchaninstructor. On catching wind of Shah Inayat, he chose to meet himand was totallytaken by his appeal and insight, concluded that he would turn into his supporter. At the point when Bulleh Shah's family had heard that he had picked an Arainas Shaikh, they ended up being irate and volunteered to persuade Bulleh Shah to leavehim and track down somebody "more commendable". Heart-broken, committed and, surprisingly, a little influenced by his family's convictions, Bulleh Shah went to ShahInayat to pronounce that he would never again be his supporter and expressedhis explanation — the lowness and the height, and the inconsistencies it introduced. Having left Shah Inayat, Bulleh Shah started to end up being increasingly confounded. His yearning and love for Shah Inayat is said to have become horrendous. He understood what a horrendous slip-up he had made and ran back to himyet ShahInayat, disappointed with his shallow and quickly moving perspectives, sent himaway. He realized he needed to redress how he had managed a tremendous signal. Bulleh Shah gone to a local area of road artists, the Kanjars and began living withjackasses. He endeavored to "become" one of them —a "most reduced" positionindividual. He lived among them and took in their moves, in the thing to himwas, something of a compensation — An upper position

Syed who was living like a Kanjar. Bulleh Shah through his poetical expressiveness arrived at the core of the commoners. He appeared to have felt extraordinary justification in this persecuted rank execution.

Shah wore Kanjar ladies' garments and started his last extraordinary dance for ShahInayat. This moving was joined by his tune — *Tere Ishq Nachaya* (Your Affectionhas Made me Dance). Detecting commitment and contrition, Shah Inayat is saidtohave pardoned him.[12]

4. Sarmad Kashani and Abhai Chand

Sarmad was born around the year 1590 in Armenia. A country sharing land-lockedwith Azerbaijan, Georgia, Turkey and Iran. Persian impacts probably serious areas of strength for been Armenia since the group of Armenian Jews that Sarmad was naturally introduced to communicated in Persian. Sarmad Kashani came froma groupof dealers, however a few practices place him in a group of rug weavers. It was the point at which each globe-trotter, skilled worker, calligrapher, vendor, voyager, weaver, writer or a Sufi from significant pieces of the then known world, barring obviously the recently "found" lands, was set out toward Hindustan. This happened in light of the fact that all of the individuals who got back fromHindustanconveyed stories of her wealth, exchange open doors, variety of beliefs, individuals, thoughts, philosophical patterns, specialties, textures and scholarly customs. Sarmad, as well, set off on his excursion of discovery.What attracted himtoHindustan was not simply business open doors. He likewise had profound interest inotherworldly matters and was quick to partake in the extraordinary philosophical discussions on the subject of the heavenly that seethed across the land. Sarmad going with an old respectable man and soon they started to speak. The elderlyperson was a Sufi and Sarmad, a Persian speaking Jew, knew all about the legends of both Christianity and Islam. consequence of the significant discussion between themwas that Sarmad switched over completely to Islam and to Sufism. At the point whenSarmad started visiting a Sufi holy place in Thatta, it was not satisfactory whether hewent alone or with the Old Sufi, however his visits were standard. He was drawntothe hallowed place since he could meet different Sufis and connect with theminconversations.

And afterward there was the music and an attractive young
fellow who came tothesanctum and sang each night. This
youthful vocalist was a Brahmin kid Abhay Chand.

[12] Bulleh Shah & Shah Inayat — Caste in 17th Century Punjab | by Dalit History Month | Medium. [online]. Available_at:_ https://dalithistorymonth.medium.com/bulleh-shah-and-shah-inayat-caste-and-religion-in-17th- century-punj-521376cfd37a..

Sarmad was astounded with him and stayed there many nights looking at AbhayChand. It wasn't some time before Abhay Chand responded the fondness and the twobecame indistinguishable.

The specific idea of the connection among Abhay and Sarmad is pretty controversial, however the memoir of Sarmad that was distributed via overseers of his sanctumout and out states that Sarmad had become hopelessly enamored with him, and that, regardless of at first contradicting their relationship, Abhay's dad at last allowed themto have a relationship.

It has been proposed that both Sarmad and Abhay Chand went to Delhi, arrivingat Shahjanabad during the 1650s. They pitched their camp close to the hospice of Khwaja Abdul Hasan, prominently known as Rabbit Bhare Saheb. Some accept that his adoration for Chand was genuine, eccentric relations being verynormal in that period and not something that was actually that censured as it later was during provincial times.[13]

5. Shah Hussian and Madholal

Shah Hussain was born in Lahore in 1538 external Taxali Door, Shah Hussainwas quite possibly of the most respected Sufi-writer, he was a contemporary of Hazrat Mian Mir and had sincere relations with Master Arjan Singh. He dedicated his life toreligion. At 36 years old years, in any case, he surrendered religion, got his facial hair and head shaved and drenched himself in dance, as the "genuine way" towards salvation.

Once, when Shah Hussain was going through Shahdara across the waterway fromLahore, his eyes fell on a kid of supreme excellence. The kid riding a pony fromShahdara, across the stream Ravi. Shah Hussain followed the kid back to his town, overpowered by the sensation of affection and charm. The holy person fell profoundlyenamored with him. Shah Hussain was then 54 years of age while the kid was just sixteen. Other than the age contrast, the kid, named Madho Lal, was a Hindu of theBrahmin rank though Shah Hussain was a Muslim of a craftsman class. (Faqri. Inthesame place). This was, as is expressed, all consuming, instant adoration. To be closeto the kid, Shah Hussain moved his home to Shahdara.

---

[13]Sarmad and Abhay Chand: A Jew and a Brahmin. [online]. Available at: https://www.dnaindia.com/analysis/column-sarmad-and-abhay-chand-a-jew-and-a-brahmin-2626139..

The elderly folks of Madho were profoundly annoyed however the adorationwas common. While it is challenging to learn the idea of his Madho Lal relationship, thewriter was blamed and thought for enjoying physical as opposed to profoundrelationship with his most vigorous devotee. They lived respectively till the demise of Shah Hussain . Their affection was serious to the point that they are presently knownby a solitary name that of Hazrat Madho Lal Hussain. They were impenetrable tothecultural resistance to their adoration. Past the individual holding of the two, ShahHussain's association with Madhu was an illustration for individuals' solidarityinSouth Asia — nullifying all strict and social organizations through their methodof life.

Significantly later, Madho Lal kept on adoring his lord and lived near his catacombfirst in Shahdara and later, after his body was unearthed because of flood immersionand reburied at the current site in Baghbanpura. Madho and Hussain lie covered next to each other in a similar nook. The sepulcher is called darbar or Regal Presence andis named Hazrat Madho Lal

Hussain; typifying one soul living in two bodies. The spring mela, respected by the Hindus, and the urs, celebrated by the Muslims, implied association and congruity among the two beliefs when joined into one festival — recalling the bond of Shah Hussain and Madhu Laal.[14]

C. Graphic Evidence

Other than imaginative confirmation, Indian history has abundant visual traces of homosexuality in India. These records exist as craftsmanship, masterpieces, models generally through the country. One such account is shielded in the asylums of Khajuraho. The Khajuraho sanctuary models, worked by the Chandela custombetween 950 to 1050 Advancement, show pictures where men open their genitals tovarious individuals are erotically embracing each other. These figures stand as anexplanation of the sexual perfection of men, women and the third gender.

Thirteenth-century Sun Temple in Konark in eastern Orissa, moreover called SuryaDevalaya, shows relative imageries, the external covered in models depicting exoticscenes from the Kamasutra.

[14] Madho Lal Hussain: Saint Of Lights. [online]. Available at: https://thefridaytimes.com/10-Jun-2022/madho-lal-hussain-saint-of-lights..

Pictures at the Buddhist passionate caves at Ajanta and Ellora, the basic perspectiveis that among the craftsmanships of Budha are certain various show-stoppers showingexciting quality and sexual scenes these masterpieces portray individuals participatingin lovemaking with a comparative sex.

Safe-havens of Puri and Tanjore in like manner portray unequivocal pictures of unusual couples. Rajrani safe-haven in Bhubaneswar has a figure depicting twowomen partaking in oral sex.[15]

D. MODERN INDIA :

The closure of Mughal time finishes and start of British empire. This period changethe historical backdrop of India as well as destroyed the legacy of the country. Also, become the one who totally condemned the homosexuality.

Presently its time when English domain comes and when the Britisher are consideringand investigating the way of life and variety of India they figured out that homosexuality in India is exceptionally normal and India are so receptive andis totally tolerating this, the Indian individuals and civilisation is methodfor modernizing and wealthy in sex related matters.

The Britishers who are the devotee of Jesus and follow the worth of chapel as findit bad and fell camouflaged about it and as attempt to forestall individuals to performsuch kind movement.

Cause as per English men scriptural idea:

Sex is for sure about children.

Male and female complete God's picture on the planet.

no other sexual association than that between a couple.

Contradicting the possibility of homosexuality by calling it a wrongdoing the peoplewho perform such thing won't get paradise it's an illness, etc and have a trepidation

[15] The Pre-Colonial History of Homosexuality in India: Why Love Is Not Western - Academike. [online]. Available at: https://www.lawctopus.com/academike/history-of-homosexuality-in-india/..

that such sort of training and culture might impact the climate of Christianityor potentially can ruin there culture as well.

They saw Indians as euphoria searching for individuals and began pushes towarddiscipline them. They expected to show European outlook among the colonizedpeople.

What's more, to force there philosophy on Indian culture In 1533 Britain lord HenryVIII passed BUGGERY ACT in which he finish up homosexuality a wrongdoingandpunished them with the death penalty (capital punishment).

The Buggery Act of 1533 declared that the 'detestable and abominable Vice of Buggery committed with mankind or beast' be punishable by death. he demonstration didn't expressly target sex between men, as it likewise appliedtohomosexuality among people and an individual with a creature. Convictions betweenpeople for homosexuality were by a long shot the most widely recognized and widelyacclaimed. Convictions under the Buggery Act 1533 were deserving of death; Later on this act was supplanted by Offenses AGAINST THE Individual Demonstration 1828.[16]

Also, later this equivalent demonstration was placed in IPC 1860 and madeSECTION 377. What's more, by this now the homosexuality is an offense in India. In the battle of homosexuality where these group of people are fighting for there right and surviving the first case registered in this section.

1. Queen empress v. kherati 1884 ILR 6 All 204,[17]

In Morarabad locale 1884, a transsexual person was captured by police after theindividual was found dressing in drag and singing with a gathering of ladies. name'Khairati' for the case, the individual became one of the first to be indicted under thescandalous section 377 of the frontier time Indian Reformatory Code (IPC), whichcondemned "bodily intercourse against the request for nature" - an umbrella termfor non-procreative sexual demonstrations. Khairati was started by the police without a

[16] Law and Oppression | Historic England. [online]. Available at: https://historicengland.org.uk/research/inclusive-heritage/lgbtq-heritage-project/law-and-oppression/..

[17] queen empress v. kherati 1884 ILR 6 All 204

complainant. They seemed to have been observing the individual who was associated with being an eunuch, driving the managing judge to compliment "thelonging of the specialists at Moradabad to really look at these untolrating weirdpractices."

II. SECTION 377 OF INDIAN PENAL CODE

Section.377- Unnatural of ences.—Whoever voluntarily has carnal intercourseagainst the order of nature with any man, woman or animal, shall be punished with1[imprisonment for life], or with imprisonment of either description for a termwhichmay extend to ten years, and shall also be liable to fine. Explanation.—Penetrationis suf icient to constitute the carnal intercourse necessary to the of ence describedinthis section.[18]

Whoever willfully has licentious intercourse against the request for nature withanyman, lady or creature, will be rebuffed.

The English thought of resistance to homosexuality got so profoundly implantedinthe Indian outlook that individuals of India began to accept that homosexualityis against Indian qualities and culture. Sadly, we failed to remember our set of experiences and keep on conveying pilgrim insight with us even after thedecriminalization of Segment 377.

The Christian qualities expressed that the reason for sexual action is to reproduce. Hence, any sexual action not implied for reproduction was untouchable. Subsequently, since multiplication naturally needs a man and a lady, sex for delight was seenas ethically undermined.

III. CASE LAWS

1. Naz foundation v. govt of India

[19]

The instance of Naz Establishment v. The Public authority of NCT of Delhi (2009) is the principal case regulations wherein section 377 of the Indian Penal Code 1860was held illegal, as it victimized the LGBTQIA+ people group of the nation anddisregarded their protection as people.

[18] Section 377. in The Indian Penal Code, 1860 ACT NO. 45 OF 1860 1* [6th October, 1860.] [19] 160 Delhi Law Times 277

This case was the main achievement in the excursion of decriminalizing Section377and giving break to the LGBTQIA+ social orders they looked for regulation, whichallowed the gay majors to engage in sexual relations.

Naz Establishment tested the legality of Section377 under Articles 14,15,19, and21of the Indian Constitution under the Delhi High Court. The establishment contendedthat section 377 of the IPC mirrors obsolete perception of sex which isn't invitedinthe public eye.

This case comprised a five judge-bench seat headed by Chief Justice Deepak Mishraand judges RF Nariman, AM Khanwilkar, DY Chandrachud, and Indu Malhotra.

The Delhi High Court presumed that section 377 of the IPC can't be utilized to rebuff two consenting grown-ups for sex, as this abuses the essential thing right to protectionwhich is an inherent component of Article 21.
The Honourable Delhi High Court likewise held that sorting individuals in light of sexdisregards another essential thing right, i.e, Article 14 of the Constitution, whichexpresses that we all, by ethicalness of being people, partake in similar basic liberties and have equivalent admittance to them.

2. Suresh Kumar Koushal & Anr vs Naz Foundation & Ors on 11 December, 2013[20]

The appeal are coordinated against judgement dated 2.7.2009 by which the Delhi High Court permitted the writ petition recorded by NAZ foundation the judgment given in Suresh Kumar Koushal and Anr versus Naz Establishment and Ors was tobesure appalling. In the above case, it was concluded that Part 377 of the IPCis naturally substantial and that homosexuality is a criminal offense in India. Thuslyit denied the established judgment of the Delhi high court in Naz Establishment v NCT. the Division bench of the Great Court neglected that a miniscule part of the country's populace is lesbians, gays, bisexuals or transsexuals and in last over 150 years under 200 people have been arraigned (according to the revealed orders) for committing

[20] Civil Appeal No. 10972 OF 2013

offense under Segment 377 IPC and this can't be made sound reason for pronouncingthat part ultra vires the arrangements of Articles 14, 15 and 21 of the Constitution.

3. Navtej Singh Johar vs Union Of India Ministry Of Law And ... on6September, 2018
[21]

It was one of the significant milestone decisions of High Court given in respect for theright of equity of LGBTQIA+ people group The people group merits equivalent privileges and regard as some other individual and oppression a person basedonsexual direction is profoundly hostile to the poise and self-esteem of the Person.

The five judges bench CJI Dipak Misra, justice A.M. Khanwilkar, justice RohintonFali Nariman, justice
D.Y. Chandrachud and justice Indu Malhotra overruled past judgment given in SureshKaushal

case and pronounced Sec 377 as unlawful as it disregarded Workmanship14,15,19 and 21 of the Constitution.

This choice established the groundwork for the Court to perceive sexual directionas apiece of individual independence under the right to privacy .Sexual direction is afundamental quality of protection. Victimization a person based on sexual directionis profoundly hostile to the respect and self-esteem of the person. Balance requests that the sexual direction of every person in the public arena should be safeguarded onaneven stage.
Navtej judgment perceived that the right to association is characteristic for Article 21of the Constitution, and 'association' doesn't only allude to marriage yet additionally'friendship,' which is physical, mental, sexual, and profound.
The Court acknowledged that Section 377 disregarded this option to lookfor consensual friendship gave under Article 21 of the Constitution.
The judgment conceptualized three remarkable ideas - transformativeconstitutionalism, constitutional morality, and the Right to Privacy.

This case was the end of victorian rule on LGBTQIA+ group over a period of 150years

[21] AIR 2018 SC 4321; W. P. (Crl.) No. 76 of 2016; D. No. 14961/2016

IV. IF RELATIONSHIP IS LEGAL THEN WHY NOT MARRIAGE

The LGBTQIA+ people group got an extraordinary triumph after the judgment of Navtej Singh Johar case as now the gay couple is permitted to live-in-relationshiphowever is that the full achievement they need is legitimizing the relationship is thearrangement of all issue, NO.

That's what the inquiry is in the event that relationship is lawful why not marriage, without marriage there is no utilization of such relationship. In a nation whereahetero couple live-in-relationship won't process effectively by the general public thenhow might a similar society acknowledge the live-in relationship of gay couple. Themain connection our general public have faith in couples is marriage.

As indicated by some review, about no less than 5-10% of populace India is anindividual from LGBTQIA+. just not many of them can let out the unadulterated truthdue to many reasons, that's what the most compelling motivations are, that even theyemerge as there personality is as yet not the solution cause yet the familyis acknowledged them however what might be said about the general public at largewhat they call themselves before them a couple with no legitimate recognization, acouple with no ability to remain before anybody, a mere people groups who permittedto live with there accomplices yet not permitted to wed them, nor ready to call thereadoration one's by such names as spouse wife as a typical hetero couple can do. A marriage is an association of two spirits to people and marriage ought tobeaccessible to couples no matter what their religion, gender, region, caste, class, variety, marriage is considered by a lot of people to be the highest quality level for commending the delight of affection and responsibility.

the isolation of hetero and gay couples into independent organizations comprises acognizable damage. Is love different for various gender? aside fromthe orientationof the individual, there is no distinction in the relationship Right to wed is a fundamental right and fundamental privileges is the freedoms of each and every residents

The presentation of same-sex marriage wouldn't dispose of this oppression same-sexwedded couples, yet it would eliminate the issue of obliviousness, and eliminate one of the reasons for bias, same-sex marriage will improve the security, confidence, well being and prosperity of LGBT individuals

Society and government are restricting the possibility of same-sex marriage byvarious reasons as by calling it an unnatural demonstration, something past the nature, illegal of nature, it will prevent and ruin and obliterate the Indian culture. Government is scrutinizing that an offspring of homo couple will become homoas well as the kid childhood was finished in that air this point looks bad as the homokidis come from hetero couple too.

Same sex marriage ought to be legitimized or not is to a greater extent a strict discussion then a political one. Getting hitched is a definitive approach to showingyour adoration and obligation to your accomplice, so for what reason should theseindividuals be denied of this right.Same-sex associations hurt nobody; one's helpor resistance to this involves individual conviction and ethical quality, with whichthepublic authority has no business to meddle.

V. NEED FOR REGISTER THE SAME SEX MARRIAGE: There are a few purposes behind that however one of the greatest is to forestall individuals to fall into Lavender marriage. "Lavender marriage" — this alludes to hetero relationships of comfort between non- hetero people — or, at any rate, one non-hetero individual —that permit the couple toevade the disgrace encompassing eccentricity and, on occasion, likewise participate inthe legitimate, social, and monetary advantages of marriage. Chiefly for gettingthe public picture of once that sort of relationships is perform.

Lavender marriage only a total extortion with each other and its likewise theinfringement the right of other to get a decent life and generally ladies' are turnedintothe prey here as a few gay men's are tie in marriage and with that they disregards theprivileges and obliterate the existence of another.

Authorizing same-sex marriage wouldn't just give legitimate acknowledgment andsecurity to LGBTQIA+ couples yet in addition advance more noteworthy social acknowledgment and diminish victimization the local area.

"Marriage is something in nature, it is not something that society creates."

Marriage is in excess of an actual association; it is likewise a profound and close tohome union.Marriage is the start — the start of the family —and is a long lastingresponsibility. It likewise gives an amazing chance to fill in magnanimity as you serveyour significant other and kids. Marriage is a bond like no other. It gives us a soul mate, a partner, as we travel through the difficulties of coexistence. youngsters arebrought up in a sound marriage, they get a fantastic view to see and experience theenduring advantages of major areas of strength for a strong family. If a normal heterosexual couple is able to enjoy such recognition and legal status insociety and able to perform every act with such ease, then why a homo couples aredeprived from such right and joy even when they are recognize as a normal personbyconstitution and also have legal validity on there presence.

Authorizing same-sex marriage is assist gay couple with partaking in the freedoms *ADOPTION, DIVORCE, INHERITENCE, PROPERTY RIGHTS, MAINTENANCE, CRUELTY etc.*

VI. COUNTRIES WHO LEGALIZE THE SAME SEX MARRIAGE

Over the world 39 nations have sanctioned the equivalent sex marriage.

Country	Year	Region	Notes
Andorra	2023	Europe	Parliament in the small mountainous country between France and Spain voted to legalize same-sex marriage.
Chile	2022	Latin America-Caribbean	Sixth South American countryto legalize same-sex marriage.
Cuba	2022	Latin America-Caribbean	Change allowing same-sex marriage was part of a broader referendum on family lawthat passed by a 66.9%to 33.1%vote.

Country	Year	Region	Notes
Mexico	2022	Latin America-Caribbean	Same-sex marriage eventually became legal nationally after the

Supreme Court declared state bans unconstitutional in 2015.

First country in formerly
Slovenia 2022 Europe
communist Eastern Europe to legalize same-sex marriage.

Nearly two-thirds of Swiss voters (64.1%) cast ballots in favor of
Switzerland 2022 Europe
legalizing same-sex marriage ina 2021 referendum.

Latin America-

Costa Rica 2020

First Central American countryto

Caribbean

legalize same-sex marriage.

Austria 2019 Europe A court ruling in 2017 eventually led to the change. Ecuador 2019 Latin America- Caribbean Court ruling made Ecuador thefifth South American countryto allow gays and lesbians to wed.

A court ruling prompted a change in the law that made Taiwanthe

Taiwan 2019 Asia-Pacific

first jurisdiction in Asia to permit gays and lesbians to wed.

Voters supported legalizing same-sex marriage by a 61.6%to 38.4%

Australia 2017 Asia-Pacific

margin in a non-binding nationwide referendum.

Finland 2017 Europe The law, passed by Parliament in
Country Year Region Notes

2014, started out as a "citizens'

Country	Year	Region	Notes
Germany	2017	Europe	initiative" – a public petition with nearly 167,000 signatures. It came into effect in 2017. Legislation passed after then-Chancellor Angela Merkel said members of her ruling Christian Democratic Union should vote their conscience even thoughthe party formally opposed same-sex marriage.
Malta	2017	Europe	Parliament almost unanimously voted to legalize same-sex marriage.
Colombia	2016	Latin America-Caribbean	Colombia's Constitutional Court legalized same-sex marriage bya 6-3 vote.
Ireland	2015	Europe	First country to legalize same-sex marriage through a popular referendum, with more than six-in ten Irish voters (62%) in favor.
Luxembourg	2015	Europe	The bill was championed bythe country's prime minister, Xavier Bettel, who is openly gay.
United States	2015	North America	Thirty-six states and the District of Columbia had legalized same-sex marriage before the U.S. Supreme Court ruled that the Constitution

Country Year Region Notes

guarantees it throughout the country.

Legal same-sex marriage took effect in Northern Ireland in 2020,

United
six years after the change in

Kingdom 2014 Europe
England and Wales. Separate legislation was enacted in Scotland in 2014.

About half of Brazil's 27
Brazil 2013 Latin America- Caribbean jurisdictions had allowed same-sex marriage until a court ruling made it legal nationwide.

Then-French President François
France 2013 Europe
Hollande signed the lawafter an unsuccessful court challenge.

First country in the Asia-Pacific
New Zealand 2013 Asia-Pacific
region to allow gays and lesbians to wed.

Second Latin American countryto
Latin America-

Uruguay 2013

legalize same-sex marriage,

Caribbean
following Argentina.

Same-sex marriage became legal
through a separate process in
Denmark 2012 Europe
Greenland, an autonomous
territory of Denmark, in 2016.

Latin America-

Argentina 2010
First country in Latin America to

Caribbean
allow gay and lesbian couples to

Country Year Region Notes

marry.

After the law took effect, the
country's prime minister at the
time, Jóhanna Sigurðardóttir, wed
Iceland 2010 Europe
her longtime partner, Jónína
Leósdóttir, becoming one of the
first people to marry under the
statute.

Measure passed by Parliament was
Portugal 2010 Europe
approved by Portugal's
Constitutional Court.

Norway 2009 Europe^{The law replaced a 1993 statute}permitting civil unions.

Gay and lesbian couples in
Sweden previously had been
Sweden 2009 Europe
allowed to register for civil unions
since 1995.

Only African country where same-
sex marriage is legal; several
South Africa 2006 Sub-Saharan Africa
countries on the continent have
passed laws that ban
homosexuality in recent years.

Same-sex marriage was legal ina
majority of Canada's provinces
Canada 2005 North America
before Parliament passed national
legislation.

Spain 2005 Europe Became the third country globally

Country Year Region Notes

to legalize same-sex marriage after
a vote in its closely divided
Parliament.

Second country in the worldto

Belgium 2003 Europe

legalize same-sex marriage, after
its neighbor, the Netherlands.

First country to legalize same-sex

Netherlands 2001 Europe

marriage after Parliament passed
the law in December 2000.

Source: Gay Marriage Around the World | Pew Research Center.[22]

And now in 2023 Nepal become the first South Asia country to legalize same-sexmarriages.

SAME-SEX MARRIAGE RATE IN DIFFERENT COUNTRY: [23]
i. In Spain, where same-sex marriage has been legal since 2005, 3.4%of the148,588 marriages registered in 2021 were same-sex – the highest share amongthe countries and territories for which data is available.
ii. The United Kingdom had the second-highest share of same-sex marriages

amongthe countries with data available, at 3.3%. However, in the UK, data is reportedfor three sub-national jurisdictions – England and Wales together, ScotlandandNorthern Ireland – rather than for the country as a whole.

iii. England and Wales, 3.5% in Scotland, and 4.2% in Northern Ireland have sincepublished marriage data for 2021, with same-sex marriage rates that year of 3.4%and 5.0%,

[22] Gay Marriage Around the World | Pew Research Center. [online]. Available at: https://www.pewresearch.org/religion/fact-sheet/gay-marriage-around-the-world/..

[23] How many marriages are same-sex in countries and territories where it's legal? | Pew Research Center. [online]. Available at: https://www.pewresearch.org/short-reads/2023/06/13/in-places-where-same-sex-marriages-are-legal- how-many-married-same-sex-couples-are-there/..

iv. The highest share of marriages between men was in Costa Rica, where theycomprised 370 of the 677 same-sex marriages (54.7%) recorded in 2022. v. In Taiwan, where 1,794 of the 2,493 same-sex marriages recorded in 2022, or 72.0%, were between two women.

vi. About 58% of couples in the nation's 980,000 same-sex households were marriedand about 42% were unmarried partners.Eleven states plus the District of Columbia had higher percentages of same-sex couple households (amongcoupled households) than the national average of 1.5%, with Washington, D.C., having the highest at 7.1%.[24]

Obviously, there is no proof from any of those nations of any of the adverse results that a portion of the rivals of same-sex marriage.

These numbers of marriage is continually increasing and showed a solid andapositive side to the nations and furthermore assist the general public with significantlyimpacting there point of view and begin thinking in another manner, and makeasegregation free environment for each part of society.

VII. BRITISHERS IDEOLOGY

What sort of rules we are adhering to at time when entire world is investigating theresociety and regulations our India so created and distant in subject on development, training, governmental issues, framework, regulations, medication and so forth. Not inthe least doing perfect in each field yet in addition way more modernize in cultural point of view and there thinking we show governmental issues, science, regulations, yet in addition show sex schooling and show such thing on no sweat many books composed regarding this matter like *Vatsyayana's Kama Sutra* and *Vedas* theseOtherworldly texts investigate the secret elements of the solidarity between the humanand the heavenly and recognize that any way that prompts understanding andacknowledgment of joy is OK including sexuality. At the point when we used to be somodernize around then what happen now due to some English monitors ran over thestream and controlled our country and not just they obliterate our way of life, variety, and school system yet additionally annihilated and, altered our outlook and thinking

[24] Census Bureau Releases Report on Same-Sex Couple Households. [online]. Available at: https://www.census.gov/newsroom/press-releases/2021/same-sex-couple-households.html..

by forcing there contemplation's and thoughts and making regulations for us byas indicated by there culture and custom.

Also, presently the bend is this, that those pilgrim society who administeredus immediately, have now even change there own guidelines and regulations as indicatedby there current point of view, yet we actually live under those obscure hovels whichwere worked by them and joyfully acknowledge there culture and standards however because of this development we sadly failed to remember our own way of life andschooling system.

Those English nations are currently becoming widely popular for there present daythinking and frameworks who are so moderate, restricted and feel sorryfor disapproved on the double, yet they change there regulations concurring with theresociety needs however we actually harvest those yields which were planted by themand presently acknowledge there regulations as our way of life and don't change it yet.

VIII. CONCLUSION

The battle to get equivalent portrayal as same as several beginnings old India the issueemerge when British Colonialism destruct the of pictures of gay articulationandsexual articulation overall turned out to be more precise and glaring. Marriage is likewise a legitimate joining of two people. Marriage shows the most groundedresponsibility you can make to each other. LGBTQIA+ individuals are similarlyas human and have similar requirements and wants as hetero people like a typical group. The contention that equivalent sex relationships ought not be made lawful "onthegrounds that they don't deliver kids" is ridiculous, then whats the point for theindividuals who wedded are above 60s or 70s as they can't create kids either stopthere marriage too. If two individuals love one another and need to join their fates, then, at that point, it is something delightful which ought to be commended. We have all the proof which shows that homosexuality lies in Indian culture fromtheVedic period to present day India yet it's not full confirmation that regardless of whether they had perform marriage however we can't overlook there presence andindividuals of that time are tolerating homosexuality effectively why not currently. However homosexuality isn't new nor is it against the Indian culture, it has consistently existed and with a lot lesser indictment The Britishers who got such regulations our country to condemning homosexualityand their relationships are presently have passed the law to sanctioned same-sex marriage in their own nation in the event that they change there regulations whynot us now is the ideal time to change such regulations for the advancement of society.

"You don't fall in love with the gender, you fall in love with a person." :- AndyBiersack

I at long last finish up by saying that homosexuality isn't an offense as it's typical as hetero couple, it is only a method of quest for satisfaction, a methodfor accomplishing sexual joy or want. Love will be love. Touching them, staying, talk, eat, seeing, them doesn't makes an individual gay or lesbian. There's positively not anobvious explanation, aside from blind bias, which forestalls LGBTQIA+ people groupgoing through a common function which will give them the freedoms and protections which hetero couples appreciate. Marriage is an indication of responsibility and love. If two men or two ladies have any desire to show that responsibility, howcauses that annihilate or harm the beliefs of marriage.

A person of this community is also brought into the world as an ordinary human. Andthey too share rights on law as we do. They also have every right to lead a normal lifein our country. And, the government should support them and not oppose them. *****

SEXUAL HARASSMENT OF WOMEN AT WORKPLACE
(Prevention, Prohibition and Redressal) Act, 2013

Authored by:- Mr Harshit Naveen and Ms Gauri Sharma.

Synopsis: -

In the modern era of the nation, we improved the quality and access the education & employment to the women. millions of Indian women are entering in the country workforce today as it is not a new evil for the women. Many working women faces sexual harassment at the workplace on the daily basis.

As it is pivotal, therefore that as a country, we endeavor to eliminate work-place sexual harassment since women have the right to work in safe and secure environment. It is the duty of every worker to ensure safety of women in a work environment and improve their participation. the participation or the contributories of the employers toward the women help in the realization of their right to gender equality and result in economic empowerment and inclusive growth and benefit the nation as a whole.

The Article has been developed with the aim to ensure that the citizens of India are aware of their rights and obligations in terms of creating safe workplace environment for women. This article reflects us commitment to empower women as economic agents and improve their ability to access markets on competitive and equitable terms. This article is of immense importance because combating sexual harassment involves developing deeper understanding of what is sexual harassment and change of attitudes in all - be it employer, employees, colleagues, friends, or policy makers.

Introduction: -

> Whereas sexual harassment results in violation of the fundamental
> rights of a Woman to equality   ”

Preamble, Sexual Harassment of Women at Workplace (Prevention, Prohibition & Redressal) Act.

"Equality of status and opportunity" must be secured for all its citizens which is briefly mentioned in the Preamble whereas right to equality under the law guaranteed by article 14 of the Indian Constitution. safer workplace is a legal right of a women. these rights are contained in the constitutional doctrine of equality under surtitle 14,15 and 21 of the Indian constitution. Articles 14,15 and 21 are the rights which are related to personal liberty & these ensure a person's right to equal protection under the law, to live a life free from preventing women from sexual harassment, discrimination, losing of personal liberty, the Convention on the Elimination of all Forms of Discrimination against Women (CEDAW), reinforced & adopted by the UN General Assembly in 1979 and which is ratified by India. Often described as an international bill of rights for women, it calls for the equality of women and men in terms of human rights and fundamental freedoms in the political, economic, social, cultural and civil spheres.

THE PRINCIPAL REASON BEHIND SEXUAL HARRESSMENT OFWOMEN AT WORKPLACE: -

Sexual harassment constitutes a gross violation of women's right to equality and dignity. It has its roots in patriarchy and its attendant perception that men are superior to women and that some forms of violence against women are acceptable. One of these is workplace sexual harassment, which views various forms of such harassment, as harmless and trivial. Often, it is excused as 'natural' male behaviors or 'harmless flirtation' which women enjoy.contraty to these perceptions, it causes serious harm and is also a strong manifestation of sex discrimination at the workplace. As today's women have their footprints in every field such as education, economics, politics, media, art, space and culture, service sectors, science and technology, etc. therefore the role of women is changed. They are working in the organizations. They shift themselves from household to commercial world. This is the main

reason behind the offensive nature of men `towards women. Men are thinks to be society as male dominated society & they do not want to be give place at the position where male exist. Males have such type of aptitude that they have complete dominion over women.

. In Favour of women of I wants to share a quote with all of you that
{"Mahari chori chore se kam h k "}.

Inspite of rising incidences of sexual harassment, their reporting is almost nil as women fear loss of personal & professional reputation and livelihood owing to the social stigma.

Enactment of the Act: [1]
For the ending of all forms of violence against women appositively impact society, hamper gender equality and constricts the social and economic development of the

country. the Government of India enact such a law for this, named Sexual Harassment of Women at Workplace (Prevention, Prohibition and Redressal) Act, 2013.

There is right to live with dignity for the women under Articles 14,15 and article 21 Of the Indian Constitution. therefore, for the elimination of such violence, discrimination on women, the act {Sexual Harassment of Women at Workplace (Prevention, Prohibition and Redressal) Act, 2013.} has been enacted by the Indian Government which is used as a preventive measure of the rights of women.

The Act is a description of the _Vishaka Guidelines_ [1] passed by the Supreme Court in 1997. The Supreme Court of India, for the first time in the Vishaka Guidelines, acknowledged Sexual Harassment at the workplace as a human rights violation. Further, the Act also reflects the commitment of the Government to the ratification of the Convention on the Elimination of all forms of Discrimination against Women

[1] https://www.legalserviceindia.com/legal/article-374-case-analysis-vishakaand-others-v-s-state-of-rajasthan.html

(CEDAW) on July 09, 1993, this new legislation makes every effort to be a user-friendly tool in the hands of the employers and employees, to create safe and secure workplaces for all women.

- "The meaning and content of the fundamental rights guaranteed in the Constitution of India are of sufficient amplitudes to encompass all facets of gender equality...."

[Late Chief Justice J.S. Verma, Supreme Court of India, Vishaka v. State of Rajasthan]

What is sexual harassment?

As such types of offences came in knowledge, or the issues evaluated to women harassment, discrimination Section 354A of the Indian Penal Code (IPC) was indeed amended in 2013 by the Criminal Law (Amendment) Act, 2013.

The amendment was made in response to the increasing concern over crimes against women and aimed to provide more stringent punishment for certain offenses.

Section 354A deals specifically with "sexual harassment" and lays down the provisions for the same. Prior to the amendment, the IPC did not have a separate section specifically addressing sexual harassment. The amendment defines sexual harassment and prescribes punishment for the offenders.

The key provisions of Section 354A of the IPC(as amended in 2013) are as follows:

1. Definition of Sexual Harassment: The section defines sexual harassment and includes actions such as unwelcome physical contact or advances, making sexually colored remarks, showing pornography, or any other unwelcome physical, verbal, or non-verbal conduct of a sexual nature.

2. Punishment: The punishment for sexual harassment is imprisonment of either description for a term that may extend to three years, or with a fine, or with both.

Earlier, there were no related laws in the Indian Penal Code that could be evoked. There were three sections in Indian Penal Code Viz. S. 94120, 354121 and 509122 to deal with such crimes. However, these related laws are framed as an offence that either amount to obscenity in public or acts that are seen to violate the modesty of women. While Section 294 IPC is a law applicable to both men and women, the latter two are specifically oriented towards women

International Laws and Policies for Addressing Sexual Harassment in The Workplace

1.1. United Nations General Assembly Resolution 48/104123 on the Declaration on the Elimination of Violence Against Women, it orders to the member of states to take measures to eliminate violence against women, protect victims, and promote gender equality and women's empowerment. It emphasizes the importance of implementing comprehensive and coordinated policies to address the root causes of violence against women and to provide support services for victims.

2.2. The Convention on the Elimination of all Forms of Discrimination against Women124(CEDAW) defines discrimination against women as any distinction, exclusion, or restriction made on the basis of sex that impairs or nullifies the recognition, enjoyment, or exercise of women's human rights and fundamental freedoms in political, economic, social, cultural, civil, or any other field.

3.3. Moreover, the Beijing Platform for Action, para. 178125, recognizes sexual harassment as a form of violence against women and as a form of discrimination, and calls on multiple actors including government, employers, unions, and civil society to ensure that governments enact and force laws on sexual harassment and that employers develop anti-harassment policies and prevention strategies.

4.4 The ILO Committee of Experts on the Application of Conventions and Recommendations plays a crucial role in promoting decent work and advancing social justice around the world. Its independent assessments help strengthen the implementation of international labor standards and contribute to improving working conditions and labor rights globally.

5.5. The International Covenant on Economic, Social and Cultural Rights contains several provisions particularly important for women. Article 7 recognizes her right to fair conditions of work and reflects that women shall not be subjected to sexual harassment at the place of work which may vitiate working environment.

Constitutional safeguards provisions against Sexual Harassment at Workplace[2]

Several constitutional safeguards and legal provisions in India are in place to address and prevent sexual harassment in the workplace. These safeguards aim to ensure a safe and respectful working environment for all employees, especially women. The primary constitutional safeguard against workplace sexual harassment in India is:

1. Right to Equality (Article 14)[3]: Article 14 of the Indian Constitution guarantees the right to equality, stating that the state shall not deny any person equality before the law or equal protection of the laws. This means that every individual, regardless of gender, has the right to be treated with equality and dignity in the workplace.

http://www.legalservicesindia.com/article/1905/sexualharassment-of-women-at-work.html
Surinder Mediratta, Handbook of Law, Women and Employment (1st ed, 2009

In addition to the constitutional provision, there is a specific law that addresses sexual harassment at the workplace In the Indian constitution it is provided that every women has the right of Every woman has a constitutional right to participate in public employment and this right is denied in the process of sexual harassment, which compels her to keep away from such employment. Sexual harassment of woman at the place of work exposes her to a big risk and hazard which places her at an inequitable position vis-à-vis other employees and this adversely affects her ability to realize her constitutionally guaranteed right under Article 19(1) (g).

Right to livelihood is an integral facet of the right to life.127 Sexual harassment is the violation of the right to livelihood. For the meaningful enjoyment of life under Article 21 of the Constitution of India, every woman is entitled to the elimination of obstacles and of discrimination based on gender. Since the 'Right to Work' depends on the availability of a safe working environment and the right to life with dignity, the hazards posed by sexual harassment need to be removed for these rights to have a meaning.

The preamble of the Constitution of India contemplates that it will secure to all its citizens – "Equality of status and opportunity." Sexual harassment vitiates this basic motive of the framers of the constitution.[4] The concept of gender equality embodied in our Constitution would be an exercise in ineffectiveness if a woman's right to privacy is not regarded as her right to protection of life and liberty guaranteed by Article 21 of the Constitution of India.

Since sexual harassment of women at the workplace violates their sense of dignity and the right to earn a living with dignity, it is absolutely against their fundamental rights and their basic human rights.

1. The Sexual Harassment of Women at Workplace (Prevention, Prohibition, and Redressal) Act, 2013: This act was enacted to provide a comprehensive legal framework for preventing and addressing sexual harassment at the workplace.

CASE LAWS RELATED TO SEXUAL HARRASMENT AT WORKPLACE OF INDIA

There are several important case laws in India that have dealt with sexual harassment at the workplace. Here are a few notable ones:

1. **Vishaka v. State of Rajasthan (1997):** Although not a case law, the Vishaka case was a landmark judgment by the Supreme Court of India that laid down guidelines to address sexual harassment at the workplace. The court held that in the absence of legislation on the matter, employers are obligated to follow these guidelines to prevent and redress sexual harassment.

2. **Apparel Export Promotion Council v. A.K. Chopra (1999):** In this case, the Supreme Court emphasized that employers have a legal obligation to provide a safe working environment that is free from sexual harassment. The court ruled that sexual harassment violates a woman's fundamental right to equality and directed employers to comply with the Vishaka guidelines.

3. **Medha Kotwal Lele v. Union of India (2013):** The Bombay High Court, in this case, expanded the scope of sexual harassment by ruling that it can occur even outside the physical premises of the workplace. The court held that if an act has a nexus with the employment or if the victim faces hostile work conditions due to such an act, it can be considered workplace sexual harassment.

4. **Pawan Kumar v. State of Haryana (2018):** In this case, the Supreme Court reiterated that sexual harassment laws must be interpreted broadly to protect women's rights. The court emphasized that workplace sexual harassment should not be limited to acts explicitly covered under the law but should also include instances that have a gendered impact on women's dignity and well-being.

- **Nipun Saxena v. Union of India (2019):** The Delhi High Court, in this case, clarified that the definition of sexual harassment includes the creation of a hostile work environment. The court held that persistent unwelcome behavior, even if it does not involve physical contact or

explicit advances, can constitute sexual harassment if it creates a hostile, intimidating, or offensive work environment for women.

These case laws, along with the Sexual Harassment of Women at Workplace Act, 2013, have played a crucial role in shaping the legal landscape concerning workplace sexual harassment in India. They provide guidance to employers, reinforce the rights of victims, and emphasize the importance of creating a safe and respectful work environment for women.

Conclusion: -

Sexual harassment of women at the workplace is a pervasive and serious issue that affects the well-being, dignity, and productivity of female employees. The consequences of sexual harassment can be devastating, leading to emotional distress, decreased work performance, and even forcing victims to leave their jobs. It is a violation of human rights and hinders gender equality in the workplace.

However, despite the existence of such laws, challenges remain in eradicating sexual harassment entirely. Many cases still go unreported due to fear of retaliation, stigma, or lack of awareness about the complaint mechanisms. Moreover, there might be cases of noncompliance by some employers, which further exacerbates the problem.

By continuing to strengthen legal frameworks, promoting awareness, and fostering a culture of zero tolerance towards sexual harassment, we can work towards a future where women can work without fear, and where workplaces are free from any form of gender-based discrimination and harassment. Ultimately, achieving this goal will not only benefit women but also contribute to a more productive, diverse, and equitable workforce overall.

THE JAN VISHWAS (AMENDMENT OF PROVISIONS) ACT, 2023- AN ATTEMPT TO IMPROVE EASE OF DOING BUSINESS IN INDIA

Authored by:- kuriachan josey

INTRODUCTION

India, with its burgeoning population and massive market potential, has long been seen as an attractive destination for foreign investment. However, the country's complex and bureaucratic business environment has often been a deterrent for companies looking to set up operations in India. In recent years, however, there have been significant efforts to improve the ease of doing business in India. Initiatives like the introduction of the Goods and Services Tax (GST) which has replaced multiple indirect taxes and has created a unified tax regime across the country, implementation of the Insolvency and Bankruptcy Code (IBC) which has expedited the resolution of insolvency cases and has provided a more predictable and robust framework for dealing with distressed businesses, digitisation of various processes and services, introduction of Labour Codes etc. has made it easier for businesses to operate.

While these efforts have undoubtedly improved the ease of doing business in India, the country continues to face challenges such as a cumbersome regulatory environment, inadequate infrastructure, and a slow judicial system. In order to address these issues and to further improve the business environment and attract more investment, the Jan Vishwas (Amendment of Provisions) Act, 2023 was passed by the parliament. The primary aim of the Act is to convert several fines to penalties and also to remove imprisonment as punishment for many offences. But the inherent aim of the Act is to improve "ease of living as well as ease of doing business" as reiterated by Commerce and Industry Minister Piyush Goyal on 22nd December 2022 in Lok Sabha while introducing Jan Vishwas Bill. The relevance of Ease of doing business in India in the current world economic scenario is noteworthy.

EASE OF DOING BUSINESS

Ease of doing business refers to the level of difficulty or ease of starting and operating a business in a particular country. The term gained importance through the popularisation of the index published by the World Bank that ranks economies on their ease of doing business, from 1-190, with a high ranking indicating a more conducive regulatory environment for local firms. The rankings are determined by sorting the aggregate scores on 10 topics, each consisting of several indicators, giving equal weight to each topic. The ease of doing business score is reflected on a scale from 0 to 100, where 0 represents the lowest and 100 represents the best performance. The factors that impact the ease of doing business include starting a business, dealing with construction permits, getting electricity, registering property, getting credit, protecting minority investors, paying taxes, trading across borders, enforcing contracts, and resolving insolvency.

Countries can improve their ease of doing business ranking by implementing reforms that make it easier for businesses to operate. The World Bank's Doing Business report annually ranks countries on the ease of doing business, and countries that improve their rankings are often motivated by the media and private sector coverage. The most improved places to do business are those that have implemented reforms that make it easier to start and operate a business. There are several success stories of countries that have significantly improved their ease of doing business ranking. For example, Singapore topped the global ranking on the ease of doing business for seven consecutive years, followed by Hong Kong SAR, New Zealand, the United States, and Denmark. China improved its position in the Doing Business ranking by almost 50 places from 78th to 31st, supported by the World Bank's technical assistance. Afghanistan, Djibouti, Côte d'Ivoire, and Togo are among the top improvers, despite being countries suffering from fragility, conflict, and violence. Rwanda has steadily climbed and maintained a high ranking for some time, currently ranking second in terms of the ease of doing business in Africa and one of only two countries in Africa that feature among the top 50 globally. India has also strived to improve its ranking and as a result, India has jumped 79 positions from 142nd in 2014 to 63rd in 2019 in World Bank's Ease of Doing Business Ranking 2020. In Order to further create a conducive environment for Industrial activities and business investment, certain provisions were included in the Jan Vishwas Act of 2023.

JAN VISHWAS ACT

The Jan Vishwas (Amendment of Provisions) Act, 2023 is expected to have a positive impact on the ease of doing business in India. The Jan Vishwas (Amendment of Provisions) Bill was first introduced in Lok Sabha on 22nd December 2022. Later, it was referred to the Joint Committee of the Parliament. The Report of the Committee was laid before the Rajya Sabha and Lok Sabha on 17th March 2023 and 20th March 2023 respectively, and the bill was passed in Lok Sabha on 27th June 2023 and Rajya Sabha on 2nd August 2023. It received the assent of the President on 11th August 2023. The Act amends 42 laws across multiple sectors, including agriculture, environment, and media and publication. The Acts being amended include the Indian Post Office Act, 1898, the Environment (Protection) Act, 1986, the Public Liability Insurance Act, 1991, and the Information Technology Act, 2000 etc. The act aims to decriminalise certain offences, reduce the compliance burden on individuals and businesses, and ensure ease of doing business. It amends 183 provisions across 42 laws to do away with imprisonment or fines for certain offences . The act provides a framework for future reforms, which is expected to further enhance the ease of doing business in India. Some of the key provisions under the Act are:

- Decriminalization of certain offences
- Reduction of compliance burden on individuals and businesses
- Ensuring ease of doing business

- Periodic revision of fines and penalties

The Jan Vishwas (Amendment of Provisions) Act, 2023 seeks to address technical and procedural lapses that have been criminalised under various laws in India. These lapses include minor defaults, technical or procedural lapses, and non-compliance with certain provisions. The criminal consequences prescribed for these lapses clog the justice delivery system and put adjudication at risk. The Act seeks to decriminalise these lapses and convert them into penalties, which will allow businesses and citizens to operate without fear of imprisonment for minor, procedural, or technical lapses. The Act is expected to bring more trust and less suspicion in the business environment and lead to a reduction in the burden on courts. Overall, the Act seeks to address technical and procedural lapses that have been criminalised under various laws in India and promote ease of doing business. Some of the implications of the Act are:

- Reduction in compliance burden: The act aims to decriminalise certain offences and reduce the compliance burden on businesses, which will make it easier for them to operate in India.
- Trust-based governance: The act is expected to promote trust-based governance and reduce the fear of imprisonment for minor, procedural, or technical lapses.
- Ease of doing business: The act is expected to promote ease of doing business in India by reducing the burden of criminal proceedings and promoting a more business-friendly environment.
- Protection from unnecessary criminalisation: The act seeks to decriminalise minor acts and convert them into penalties, which will protect citizens from unnecessary criminalisation for minor, procedural, or technical lapses.
- Reduction in the burden on courts: The act is expected to reduce the burden on courts by converting minor offences into penalties and reducing the number of criminal proceedings.

Even though the Jan Vishwas (Amendment of Provisions) Act, 2023 is expected to have a positive impact on the ease of doing business in India; there are some key challenges in implementing the Act. Some of the challenges are:

- Resistance from stakeholders: Some stakeholders may resist the implementation of the Act, as it may affect their interests. For example, manufacturers of substandard drugs may not want to be fined instead of being imprisoned.
- Lack of clarity: The Act amends 42 laws across multiple sectors, which may lead to confusion and lack of clarity in implementation.
- Capacity building: The implementation of the Act may require capacity building of the judiciary, law enforcement agencies, and other stakeholders.
- Constitutional challenge: The Jan Vishwas Act has been challenged on the grounds that it creates "adjudicatory officers" within the bureaucracy with the authority to impose penalties, which may be a violation of the separation of

powers.

- Enforcement: The enforcement of the Act may be a challenge, as it requires a change in the mindset of the stakeholders and a shift towards trust-based governance.

CONCLUSION

In conclusion, while India's business environment has historically been challenging, there have been significant improvements in recent years. The government's focus on simplifying regulations, implementing key reforms, and digitizing processes has made it easier for companies to do business in India. The enactment of the Jan Vishwas (Amendment of Provisions) Act, 2023 is the latest step in this process. However, further efforts are needed to address the remaining challenges and create a truly conducive environment for investment and economic growth in India.

INDIAN SURROGACY LAWS AND THEIR LACUNAS

-by Kirti Bedi[1], Ashish[2] and Rachita Sharma[3]

"Surrogacy is a path to cherish parenthood when rest of the paths seem invisible"

Surrogacy is a practice whereby the human gametes of the intending couple are fertilized together through the In-vitro fertilization technique and then a fertilized egg, an embryo, is placed in another woman's reproductive organs who is termed as the surrogate mother. Later on, the surrogate mother gives away the child to intending parents who raise the child. Eventually, the child is deemed to be a biological child of intending parents and hence is made titled to all the rights or privileges of a natural child. Surrogacy developed as an assisted reproductive technique between the years 1975 to 1985, around the globe. The Indian people soon adopted this technique and hence surrogacy was legalized in 2002. The Indian Council for medical research developed the guidelines for surrogacy which were then approved by GOI in 2005. Subsequently, India became a surrogacy hub for nationals and non-nationals and as a result, UN declared the India the *"world capital for surrogacy"* in 2012. It was also named the *"cradle of the world.* Though surrogacy gained popularity in India, it lacked laws to govern it which enticed grave ethical and legal issues such as child trafficking, exploitation of surrogates, forcing women to be surrogates and many more. To control such unethical practices, parliament banned commercial surrogacy in 2015 and aimed at regulating surrogacy through statutes. Then, in 2021 parliament enacted Surrogacy (Regulation) Act, 2021,and Assisted Reproductive Technology (Regulation) Act, 2021 which now governs surrogacy. This paper aims to detect the lacunas in the Indian surrogacy laws such as the exclusion of the LGBTQ+ community and single parents, vague conditions for being surrogate mothers, essentiality certificates invading privacy rights, and so on.Furthermore, it aims to suggest some changes which can be made to the existing laws.

Keywords – surrogacy, Indian surrogacy laws, Surrogacy (Regulation) Act 2021, Assisted Reproductive Technology, Lacunas in surrogacy Laws.

INDIAN SURROGACY LAWS AND THEIR LACUNAS

INTRODUCTION

Surrogacy is the path to cherish parenthood when the rest of the paths seem invisible. In other words, couples who cannot have a child by standard or regular methods opt for surrogacy. In the surrogacy method, the surrogate mother carries the child in her womb for the intending parents. The word surrogate has its origin in the Latin word *"surrogatus"* which is a past participle of the word *"surrogare"*. Surrogare means a substitute that is when a person is appointed to act in place of another person. This is because the surrogate is a woman who bears the child in the place of another woman, either from her egg or from the eggs of the intending parents.

The surrogacy methods evolved by the evolving technology around the globe. It is an Assisted Reproductive Technology that evolved as a boon for infertile couples. Surrogacy helps them to create a family and gain respect in society. In a country like India, where patriarchal mindsets prevail freely, having a child is a matter of respect and procreation is a way of getting socially accepted. Also, it fulfills the desire of the couple to enjoy the parental journey by way of surrogacy.

Slowly the world started accepting it and as a result,the world's first IVF boy, *Louise Joy Brown* was born in Great Britain on July 25, 1978.Two months later, the world's second and India's first IVF (in vitro fertilization) baby, *Kanupriya alias Durga* was born in Kolkata on October 3, 1978. Thereafter, surrogacy practices started prevailing in India. As a result, surrogacy was legalized in India in 2002. Gradually, surrogacy became a legal issue as it led to many illegal and immoral practices such as child trafficking, exploitation of women, abandonment of children, forcing women to provide for surrogacy services, and so on. Taking note of it, the government banned commercial surrogacy in India in 2015.

Before 2015, the ICMR (Indian Council of Medical Research) regulated the operation of Surrogacy in India. It issued guidelines on Surrogacy and Assisted Reproductive Technology in 2005. Later on, in 2009, the Law Commission released the 228th Law Commission Report which recommended the prohibition of commercial surrogacy and legalizing altruistic surrogacy in India. It also emphasized creating legislation on surrogacy. Also, the case of **Manji Yamada** *v.* **Union of India & Ors.**[4]and the case of **Jan Balaz** *v.* **Anand Municipality & Ors.**which are considered landmark cases of Surrogacy, impacted the government and generated the need for making legislation on Surrogacy.

Further, in 2021, the centre enacted two pieces of legislation that now govern surrogacy in India. These were Surrogacy (Regulation) Act, 2021, and Assisted Reproductive Technology, 2021. The Surrogacy Act completely prohibited Commercial Surrogacy and legalized altruistic surrogacy.

As soon as they got enacted, they became a topic of discussion in the legal fraternity. The laws invite a discussion over the various fundamental rights of an individual and other complexities. This paper is centered on the issues of the Surrogacy Act and seeks to provide probable solutions for the same.

GENERAL INTRODUCTION TO SURROGACY (REGULATION) ACT, 2021

Section – 2(zd) of the Surrogacy (Regulation) Act, 2021 as follows:

Section 2(zd): *"Surrogacy" means a practice whereby one woman bears and gives birth to a child for an intending couple with the intention of handing over such child to the intending couple after the birth;*

Surrogacy is defined as a practice under which one woman bears and gives birth to a child with the intention to relinquish the child to intending parents after the birth. The Act provides that a child born out of surrogacy will be deemed as a biological child of the intending parents and shall have all the rights and privileges of a natural child.

To avail of the surrogacy, the intending parents shall have the essentiality certificate along with the eligibility certificate. The surrogate mother shall also need to have the eligibility certificate. (Section – 4).

The act also establishes some authorities to regulate and govern surrogacy and assisted reproductive technologies. These authorities are:

(i)   National Assisted Reproductive Technology and Surrogacy Registry– constituted under Section 15 of the Act – for the registration of Surrogacy clinics

(ii)   National Assisted Reproductive Technology and Surrogacy Board – constituted under Section 17 of the Act – functions of the board provided u/s 25

(iii)   State Assisted Reproductive Technology and Surrogacy Board – constituted under Section 26 of the Act – functions of the board provided u/s 26

(iv)   Appropriate Authority - constituted under Section 35 of the Act – functions of the board provided u/s 36

It mainly prohibits the following act:

(i)   Prohibition to abandon child born through surrogacy – Section 7

(ii)   Prohibition of Abortion – Section 10 – no one shall force the surrogate to abort the child

(iii)   Prohibition on Commercial surrogacy, exploitation of surrogate mothers and children born out of surrogacy – Section 38

Punishment provisions are covered under sections 38 – 41. It also provides for punishment in case someone continues to do the prohibited act.

LACUNAS IN SURROGACY LAWS

In India, every statute is made in conformity with the Constitution of India which is the supreme law of the land. Further, the law implemented should be relevant to the present legal and social scenario of the country. There are a lot of times when the centre has failed to comply either with both or one of the conditions. When such a law is implemented, it gives rise to many legal and social complications. A similar situation can be seen with the Surrogacy (Regulation) Act, 2021 which is either in contravention of the Constitution of India or lacks societal advancement. Some of the major lacunas in the law are discussed below:

1. **EXCLUDED CLASSES**

The Surrogacy (Regulation) Act, 2021 only allows married couples and single women who are either widows or divorced to opt for surrogacies. It implies that the legislature aimed to exclude a lot of classes from the purview of surrogacy.

The debate initiates with the exclusion of **unmarried women** from opting the surrogacy as their reproductive choice. In India, every woman is entitled to have a reproductive choice which is a dimension of personal liberty under Article 21. In the case of **Suchita Srivastava & Ors.**v.**Chandigarh Administration**[5], the apex court held that *"there is no doubt that a woman's right to make reproductive choices is also a dimension of 'personal liberty' as understood under Article 21 of the Constitution of India. It is important to recognize that reproductive choices can be exercised to procreate as well as to abstain from procreating. The crucial consideration is that a woman's right to privacy, dignity, and bodily integrity should be respected.* Abstaining unmarried women to choose surrogacy as a way of reproduction is a clear denial of the reproductive choice of a woman which intervenes with her liberty and violates Article 21. In addition to this, the Act prima facie discriminates between women who are widows or divorced and unmarried. If observed wisely, the act is only allowing surrogacy to those women who are either married or who have been once in a marital relationship. This act depicts the patriarchal behavior of the state which consecutively violates Article 14. The right to reproductive choice should not discriminate between married and unmarried women. In the case of **X. v. The Principal Secretary, Health and Family Welfare Department, Govt. of NCT of Delhi and Ors**[6], the Supreme Court held that *the rights of reproductive autonomy, dignity, and privacy under Article 21 give an unmarried woman the right of choice on whether or not to bear a child, on a similar footing of a married woman.*

The law also denies surrogacy to **single men** including divorced or widowers. Herein the state has discriminated based on gender because it not only excludes unmarried single men but also widowers and divorced men. This violates Articles 14 & 15 as the state has not only denied equality to the citizens but also discriminated against them based on gender. As a matter of human rights, every human has a right to live with dignity and liberty, including procreating and having a family of one's choice and denying men from opting for surrogacy as a way to procreate and have a family violates the human rights of men. Also, this depicts the substantial interference of the state in one's way of living leading to the violation of the constitutional policy.

The Act only allows surrogacy for married couples and excludes **Live-in relationship couples** from opting for surrogacy as a way to procreate. The Supreme Court has recognized live-in relationships' legality in several cases which makes the exclusion of these couples a matter of debate.

The Act bars the **LGBTQ+ community** from making reproductive choices and opting for surrogacy as a way of procreating. Though the state does not recognize same-sex marriage, the apex court in its judgment decriminalized the homosexual act by striking down Section 377 of the Indian Penal Code and held that *"LGBT persons, like other heterosexual persons, are entitled to their privacy, and the right to lead a dignified existence, without fear of persecution. They are entitled to complete autonomy over the most intimate decisions relating to their personal life, including the choice of their partners. Such choices must be protected Under Article 21. The right to life and liberty would encompass the right to sexual autonomy and freedom of expression."*[7] Also, in the case of **Manji Yamada**v. **Union of India & Ors.**[8], the court went to the extent of observing that *alternatively, the intended parent may be a single male or a male homosexual couple.*[9] This landmark case on surrogacy included a brave remark on the LGBTQ+ community even before it was even an issue in India. Though same-sex relations are still not widely accepted by Indian society, the community was given the right to sexual autonomy and a right to choose a partner of their own choice then they should also be entitled to lead a family as per their choice and the state should abstain from interfering in the private spheres of people's lives. The LGBTQ+ community is coming forward and demanding its rights. Currently, the writ petition[10] for the recognition of the right of same-sex couples to marry is pending before the Supreme Court of India. Sooner or later, the community will come forward to demand the right to reproductive choice and the right to have a family because they have got sturdy constitutional backing of Articles 14 and 21. The exclusion of the community violated Article 14 as the state has denied the equality treatment to the citizens. Further, the provisions violate Article 21 for the reason that provisions deny personal liberty to this particular community by denying to opt for surrogacy as a way to procreate.

The next excluded classes bar **foreign couples** to opt for surrogacy treatment in India. Only people of Indian Origin are legally allowed to opt for surrogacy. Though there is no such issue involved with the exclusion of foreign couples from the surrogacy act, it only brings India's position where it was before 2002.

The exclusion of all these classes is a straightforward indication of the patriarchal mindset of the state and the excessive interference of the state in the private lifestyles of the citizens. The relevant provisions violate the constitutional policy and basic structure of the constitution in different aspects.

2. MEDICAL CERTIFICATE INVADING FUNDAMENTAL RIGHTS

Section 4(iii)(a)(I) of the Surrogacy Act provides that to get the essentiality certificate the intending parents need to get a certificate of a medical indication necessitating the gestational surrogacy. The necessary conditions to obtain such a certificate have not been defined anywhere in the act but the prima facie reading of the provision gives an impression that the necessary condition refers to the infertility of either of the parents or both of the parents. The Act only allows surrogacy, in case the parents are infertile. This provision invades fundamental rights in a two-fold manner.

(i)   Medical certificate invading privacy rights

This very provision invites a discussion over the privacy rights of intending parents or women. Openly showcasing or sharing information about their infertility can harm the right to privacy of the parents. The case of **Justice K. S. Puttaswamy (Retd.) & Anr. v. Union of India & Ors**[11] held that the right to privacy is a fundamental right under Article 21 of the Indian Constitution. The infertility certificate depicts the personal information of an individual and in general, individuals are reluctant to share such private information with others. The Act makes it necessary for the intending parents to get a medical certificate that necessitates surrogacy which is equivalent to compelling the individuals to share private information about themselves with the authorities.

The scope of privacy rights is no more limited to the right of being left alone, the judiciary has evolved the concept of privacy to broader aspects. The landmark judgment on the right to privacy has affirmed three aspects of the fundamental right to privacy, namely intrusion with an individual's physical body, informational privacy, and privacy of choice.

The individuals hold informational privacy over their private data or information which can only be shared as per the consent of the individuals. Though the right to privacy is not absolute in nature, the restrictions must be just, fair, and reasonable. Any arbitrary restriction over privacy rights will be construed as a violation of the fundamental rights of an individual. However, the information about the infertility of a human being is private in nature and the state shall abstain from compelling individuals to publicize such information. This condition has also limited the scope of surrogacy to infertile individuals.

(ii)   Medical certificate invading right to make reproductive choices

Though the right to make reproductive choices has been mainly viewed as a women-centric issue, this is an issue common to all humans. Every human being holds a right to reproduce irrespective of gender and sexual identity. The right to reproduce or the right to make a reproductive choice is more of a human right that should also be inclusive of choosing the way by which one wants to reproduce. Herein, the medical certificate is only given to those who are infertile and could not bear a child due to medical complications. The Act has ignored the marital relationships in which one of the partners suffers from the STDs and also the people who have no health issues and are not willing to go for standard pregnancies. The unwillingness could arise for uncountable reasons, some of them could be the nuclear families, women being the sole earning members, professional requirements, etc. The second condition has been identified by the Supreme Court in the case of **Manji Yamadav. Union of India & Ors.**[12] The court observed that *a female intending parent may also be fertile and healthy, but unwilling to undergo pregnancy.*[13] Hence, the condition of the medical certificate denies the right of reproductive choice to the fertile intending parents or woman.

3.   BAR ON TRADITIONAL METHOD OF SURROGACY.

There are two types of surrogacies based on the relation of the Surrogate with the child. These two types are:

(i)   Traditional Method of Surrogacy

In the case of **Manji Yamadav. Union of India & Ors.**[14], Supreme Court defined traditional surrogacy and stated that *in "traditional surrogacy" (also known as the Straight method) the surrogate is pregnant with her own biological child, but this child was conceived with the intention of relinquishing the child to be raised by others; by the biological father and possibly his spouse or partner, either male or female. The child may be conceived via home artificial insemination using fresh or frozen sperm or impregnated via IUI (intrauterine insemination), or ICI (intra-cervical insemination) which is performed at a fertility clinic.*[15]

The act does not define the traditional method of Surrogacy but it merely means that the eggs of the surrogate mother are fertilized with the sperm of the father or the sperm donor by the way of IVF or Intrauterine Insemination. The Surrogacy Act puts a bar on the traditional method of surrogacy i.e., the surrogate cannot be an egg donor.

(ii)   Gestational method of Surrogacy

The court also defined Gestational Surrogacy in this case. it stated that *in gestational surrogacy" (also known as the Host method) the surrogate becomes pregnant via embryo transfer with a child of which she is not the biological mother. She may have made an arrangement to relinquish it to the biological mother or father to raise, or to a parent who is themselves unrelated to the child (e. g. because the child was conceived using egg donation, germ donation, or is the result of a donated embryo). The surrogate mother may be called the gestational carrier.* In the Surrogacy Act, gestational surrogacy has been defined in the explanation clause of Section – 4(ii)(a). It states that*"for the purposes of this sub-clause and item (I) of sub-clause (a) of clause (iii) the expression "gestational surrogacy" means a practice whereby a surrogate mother carries a child for the intending couple through implantation of embryo in her womb and the child is not genetically related to the surrogate mother"* The gestational method allows the parent to either transfer the embryo made with the fertilization of their gametes or the embryo made with the fertilization of donor's gametes which means the parents can be unrelated from the child. The Act only allows gestational surrogacy which means the surrogate mother is barred from donating her eggs for surrogacy.

The Act not only bars the surrogate from donating the gametes but also denies intending parents to use the gametes of the other donors. Currently, a case[16] is pending the Supreme Court in which the various provision has been challenged by the petitioners on which the centre has issued clarifications[17]. One such clarification issued was that the surrogate mother need not be genetically related to the child but the child must be genetically related to the intending parents. The ambiguity arose from the Section – 2(zg) of the Surrogacy Act, 2021 which states that *"surrogate mother" means a woman who agrees to bear a child (who is genetically related to the intending couple or intending woman) through surrogacy from the implantation of embryo in her womb and fulfils the conditions as provided in sub-clause (b) of clause (iii) of Section 4.* There was ambiguity regarding the expression *"who is genetically related to the intending couple or intending woman."* This expression gave the impression that it conveys that the surrogate mother should be genetically related to the child. Later on, the same was clarified by the state in the Supreme Court.

This clarification further led to the conclusion that the child should only be genetically related to the parents and not to donors, neither surrogate nor any other donor. The favorable view is that the maximum number of times parents avail of the option of surrogacy as a last resort and they have already gone through the failed results of IVF and intrauterine insemination. They have allowed using the donor's gametes throughout the process then denying the same at a later stage makes the law unreasonable. The law is also conflicting with the Assisted Reproductive Technology (Regulation) Act, 2021 which allows the use of donor's gametes for reproduction through the use of assisted reproductive technology and surrogacy is one of them. Also, there can be chances when the parents are unfit for using their gametes in procreating hence traditional surrogacy should be allowed and there should be no bar on using the gametes of a donor for surrogacy purposes.

4. BAR ON COMMERCIAL SURROGACY

Surrogacy can further be divided into two forms based on the monetary value provided to the surrogate. The two forms are:

(i)   Commercial Surrogacy

Commercial Surrogacy has been defined in the Surrogacy Act under Section 2(g).

Section 2(g): *"Commercial surrogacy" means commercialisation of surrogacy services or procedures or its component services or component procedures including selling or buying of human embryo or trading in the sale or purchase of human embryo or gametes or selling or buying or trading the services of surrogate motherhood by way of giving payment, reward, benefit, fees, remuneration or monetary incentive in cash or kind, to the surrogate mother or her dependents or her representative, except the medical expenses and such other prescribed expenses incurred on the surrogate mother and the insurance coverage for the surrogate mother"*

Commercial Surrogacy refers to providing surrogacy services in exchange for money. The Surrogacy Act completely bars commercial surrogacy in any manner which means no monetary value should be provided to the surrogate except the medical expenses and insurance coverage. This has been done to prevent the abuse and exploitation of women by their family members, middlemen, or Surrogacy agencies. The government realized that commercial surrogacy became the way to the trafficking of children. This was the reason behind the banning of commercial surrogacy in India in 2015.

(ii)   Altruistic Surrogacy

Altruistic Surrogacy is defined under Section – 2(b) of the Surrogacy Act.

Section 2(b): *"Altruistic surrogacy" means the surrogacy in which no charges, expenses, fees, remuneration or' monetary incentive of whatever nature, except the medical expenses and such other prescribed expenses incurred on surrogate mother and the insurance coverage for the surrogate mother, are given to the surrogate mother or her dependents or her representative.*

The Act only allows altruistic surrogacy i.e., no monetary benefits shall be provided to the surrogate except for the medical expenses and insurance coverage.

According to the Act, the surrogate shall not be provided with any monetary benefits but this provision arises the issues in two ways:

(i)   Difficulties in finding a surrogate

In this modern era, humans always look for an opportunity to gain benefits which can be monetary or non-monetary. The question arises that if no monetary benefits can be provided to the surrogate, then why would she agree to suffer the pain caused during pregnancy or face the drastic changes that occur during pregnancy? The woman goes through many bodily and lifestyle changes during pregnancy and post-pregnancy. It is really difficult to find any woman who does it for free and only for the sake of relinquishing the child to the indenting parents. It is very difficult for the intending parents to search and look out for such a woman who agrees to provide surrogacy services in exchange for no monetary benefits. Middle-class or upper-class women will hardly agree to do so because such complicated things are generally avoided by them. It is difficult to say that they would agree to do so for money and as far as the lower-class or poor-class women are considered they will only agree to be a surrogate for monetary purposes only because all they need in life is money to survive. The bar on commercial surrogacy makes it impossible for the intending parents to find a surrogate mother who could provide the service without asking for any money.

(ii)   Exploitation of women's ability to reproduce

Even if the first issue is somehow resolved by the indenting parents and they can find a surrogate who agrees to be a surrogate mother of their child without asking for any monetary compensation still the act itself will be equal to exploiting the women's ability to carry a child in her womb. The woman goes through a drastic change in her body during the pregnancy whether its standard pregnancy or pregnancy by way of assisted reproductive technologies hence if a woman is going through the changes, she is entitled to get monetary compensation because in the end she will be left with nothing, neither the child nor any money but only with the post-partum complications. Though the act provides for insurance coverage for post-partum complications, it's not necessary that she will go through such drastic complications which are covered by the insurance policy. There could be minor inconveniences caused which are not covered under the insurance policies and many minor needs can arise which can only be resolved or fulfilled by way of monetary compensation. Hence, any woman who provides surrogacy services should be entitled to monetary compensation.

The main focus should be on minimizing child trafficking and exploitation of women and not on eradicating the commercial element involved in surrogacy.

5. VAGAUE CONDITIONS FOR BEING A SURROGATE

The act provides for many conditions precedent for being a surrogate mother but the conditions around which the issue involves are the following:

(i)   Marital status

Section – 4(iii)(b)(I) states that only the woman who is ever married can be a surrogate. The provision makes it even more difficult for the intending parents to find a woman who has been married.

(ii)   Should be a mother

Section – 4(iii)(b)(I) also states that the surrogate shall have a child of her own. No woman who has a child of her own will ever agree to be a surrogate that too for altruistic purposes this is so because the woman is already engaged in her motherhood duties and other duties.

The reason behind enacting this provision could be to maintain the social acceptance of the women who opt to be the surrogate because in India, being a surrogate is not viewed as something respectful but the women have to face constant criticism from society for the same. Often, families deny accepting such girls as wives or daughters – in law who have delivered a baby before marriage. The condition for having children could be to avoid complications that can occur in the pregnancy after the woman has been delivered from the surrogacy. Though these provisions have been enacted with a view to protect the dignity of a woman and to maintain the social acceptance of surrogate mothers, these provisions have only made it difficult for the intending parents to find a woman who is married and has a child. Also, the decision to be a surrogate should be of a woman and her opinion should matter rather than the opinion of society. If the state continues to enact such provisions, then society will never abstain from criticizing women for their choices in life and will never accept the service of surrogate mothers as a matter of honor and not as a matter of disrespect.

SUGGESTIONS

1. The state should consider the inclusion of unmarried women, single men, live-in couples, and the LGBTQ+ community under the Act so that they can avail of the option of surrogacy and should not deny the right to reproduce and the right to make reproductive choices.

2. The state should consider making surrogacy available to people who desire to reproduce by way of surrogacy and should not just restrict it to infertile couples. Also, privacy issues should be considered.

3. The state can make arrangements to prioritize the donors in case the parents cannot use their gametes for surrogacy. It can also allow traditional surrogacy in

case nothing else works for parents or in rare conditions to avoid the emotional attachment of the surrogate mother with the child.

4. The state needs to treat commercial surrogacy as a contract and to avoid immoral practices, the state can scrutinize the procedures and can keep a regular check on the well-being of the baby after its birth for a considerable period. The state should focus more on eradicating immoral or illegal practices rather than prohibiting commercial surrogacy.

5. The state can also consider easing the conditions for being a surrogate so that the intending parents can find the surrogate.

CONCLUSION

The whole article depicts that Surrogacy has become a widely accepted practice in India which led to the creation of legislation namely the Surrogacy (Regulation) Act, 2021. The government took steps to govern and regulate surrogacy by way of legislation but has used its powers extensively. Consecutively, the act does not fit well as per currently prevailing constitutional and legal norms. This act is a result of the patriarchal and outdated thinking of the parliament. As even unmarried females and single men are kept outside the purview of the act. The state should look forward to amending the provisions of the act to keep it in conformity with the present constitutional and legal norms. Though various provisions of the Surrogacy Act have been challenged in the case of **Arun Muthuvel** *vs.* **Union of India**[18], the state can also consider amending the present legislation. The state needs to make surrogacy more hassle-free rather than making it difficult for the intending parents. The surrogacy law should evolve in a way that an individual can easily avail of the surrogacy method. Making it hard will only lead to illegal practices. One of the objectives to enact the legislation was to curb illegal and immoral practices and to achieve the objectives of the act, the state needs to ease the conditions precedent to avail surrogacy. Otherwise, there is a probability that individuals can indulge in illegal practices to avail of surrogacy. Eventually, to attain the objectives of the surrogacy law, the state can amend the law in a manner to conforms it with the constitutional and legal norms. Amendments by the state and interpretation by Supreme Court and High Courts are the only way to improve the Surrogacy Act.

THE LAW FOR COSUMER IN INDIA

MR. ARUN KUMAR*
DR. RITU SINGH MEENA**
CHINMAY KAUSHIK***

Abstract

In a complex economy like India, where the network of traders and consumers is emerging at a rapid pace, and the existing traders are moving towards expansion, and the nation is also inviting various industrial institutions to be a part of the Indian economy, it directs us to focus more on the betterment of the consumer and trader relationship. Here, the traders are well-focused and not making any deficiencies or infringements to the rights of the consumer. Additionally, the consumer needs to be satisfied while also keeping in mind their duties.

This emergence of commerce and trade practices necessitates awareness and empowerment of consumers, as well as protection from any kind of unfair trade practices and deficiencies in service. In the year 2019, the Consumer Protection Act was enacted with the objective to provide better protection of the interests of consumers and to make provisions for the establishment of consumer protection councils and other authorities for settling consumer disputes.

Although we have made many technological developments that enhance the quality, accessibility, efficacy, and availability of goods and services, even today a large number of consumers are vulnerable victims of unscrupulous exploitation through unfair trade practices. The main reason behind these exploitations is the lack of awareness and consumer empowerment. Even after the act comes into force, there is still a large majority of consumers for whom their rights and duties remain incomprehensible, making consumer awareness and empowerment the utmost requirement for economic growth. This chapter aims to detail all the necessary points to facilitate consumers, making it comprehensible for consumers in India.

Keywords: Consumer, Redressal Agency, Goods, Defect, Exploitation.

*Assistant Professor at Maharishi Law School, Maharishi University of Information Technology, Noida, India.
** Assistant Professor at Maharishi Law School, Maharishi University of Information Technology, Noida, India.
***Student at Maharishi Law School, Maharishi University of Information Technology, Noida, India

Introduction

"Consumer is the king" said Mahatma Gandhi, and to remove the helplessness of that consumer we require protecting the interest of the consumers against unscrupulous exploitations. The consumer is the purpose of the business, he is not an outsider but a part of it, the whole business depends on the consumer as he is the one who is giving them an opportunity to carry on the trade practices. The satisfaction of the consumers lies in the hands of the business and how much extra miles it can go to completely satisfy its customers and handle their grievances. To systematically organize the consumer sector, required a law that enables consumers to make informed choices; ensures fair, equitable, and consistent outcomes for consumers; and facilitates timely and effective grievance redressal. To empower consumers through awareness and education; enhance consumer protection and safety through progressive legislations and prevention of unfair trade practices; enable quality and quantity assurance through standards and their conformance; and ensure access to affordable and effective grievance redressal mechanisms. The Consumer Protection Act 1986 was later amended by The Consumer Protection Act 2019.

The objectives of the act were also discussed in the landmark case of Dr. J.J. Merchant v. ShrinathChaturvedi,[19]**The main objectives of the act are to provide speedy and simple redressal to consumer disputes, to set up the Consumer Dispute Redressal**
Commission at the district, state, and national levels, To render simple, inexpensive, and speedy remedies to the consumers. These quasi-judicial bodies have to observe the principles of natural justice and have been empowered to provide reliefs of specific nature and look after the appropriate compensations and penalties, hear complaints against defective goods and deficient services, and protect a large body of consumers from exploitation.

Brief Introduction the Consumer Protection Act 2019
Before thisConsumer Protection Act 2019 came into force *The Consumer Protection Act 1986* **was in force which, for a long time governed and regulated the consumer sector but it also held some shortcomings in it, which were needed to be resolved and the provisions needed to be made for clear and effective governance and regulation and many other things also were there to be added as the trade and commerce sector was also moving towards the expansion and globalization it was essential for the improvements in the existing law in 1986. Later in the year 2011, a bill, to amend the** *Consumer Protection Act 1986,* **however, due to the dissolution of the Lok Sabha the bill lapsed. Later in the year 2015 and 2018 also**

introduced but couldn't make it into the enforcement. Finally, a new bill with a lot more changes and innovative features such as *product liability, setting up the central consumer protection authority, provisions for misleading advertisements, and more improvements in the functioning of the consumer judicature,* named The Consumer Protection Bill was introduced in Lok Sabha and was passed and in the year 2020 on 20th July,*The Consumer Protection Act 2019* came into force. This Act extends to the whole of India and this Act shall apply to all goods and services[20]

<u>Objectives of the Act :</u>

- To eradicate the consumer's ignorance and make them aware of their rights.
- To efficiently organize the unorganized consumer sector at a large scale.
- To put a full stop to the widespread consumer exploitation.

Who is a"Consumer"?

The word "consumer" in a basic implied sense means a person who consumes. According to Sec. 2(7) of *The Consumer Protection Act 2019,* "any person who purchases any goods for consideration or, hires or avails any services or any other person who uses the purchased goods and services, on the approval of the original buyer of the goods is termed as a consumer".[21]

The word "consumer" does not include the person who purchases the goods for further production or reselling purposes or any other kind of commercial purposes. A consumer is the ultimate enjoyer of the goods and he does not use the purchased goods for other commercial purposes.

Other important definitions

"**<u>Defect</u>**" defined under sec.2(10) means,"any fault, imperfection, or shortcoming in the quality, quantity, potency, purity or standard which is required to be maintained by or under any law for the time being in force or under any contract, express or implied, or as is claimed by the trader in any manner whatsoever in relation to any goods or product and the expression "defective" shall be construed accordingly".[22]

"**<u>Deficiency</u>** " is defined under sec.2(11) means,"any fault, imperfection, shortcoming, or inadequacy in the quality, nature and manner of performance which is required to be maintained by or under any law for the time being in force or has been undertaken to be performed by a person in pursuance of a contract or otherwise in relation to any service and includes— (*i*) any act of negligence or omission or commission by such person which causes loss or injury to the consumer; and

(*ii*) Deliberate withholding of relevant information by such person to the consumer".[23]

"**Goods**" defined under sec.2(21) means,"every kind of movable property".[24]

"**Service**" defined under sec.2(42) means,"service of any description which is made available to potential users banking, financing, insurance, transport".[25]

"**Product Liability**" defined under sec.2(34) means,"the responsibility of a product manufacturer or product seller, of any product or service, to compensate for any harm caused to a consumer by such a defective product manufactured or sold or by a deficiency in services relating thereto".[26]

"**Restrictive Trade Practice**" defined under sec.2(41) means , "a trade practice that tends to bring about manipulation of price or its conditions of delivery or to affect the flow of supplies in the market relating to goods or services in such a manner as to impose on the consumer's unjustified costs or restrictions and shall include--

(*i*) delay beyond the period agreed to by a trader in the supply of such goods or in providing the services which have led or are likely to lead to a rise in the price;

(*ii*) any trade practice which requires a consumer to buy, hire or avail of any goods or, as the case may be, services as a condition precedent for buying, hiring, or availing of other goods or services".[27]

"**UnfairTradePractices**" defined under sec.2(47) means, " a trade practice which, to promote the sale, use or supply of any goods or for the provision of any service adopts any unfair method or unfair or deceptive practice including any of the following practices, namely:—

(*i*) making any statement, whether orally or in writing or by visible representation including through electronic record, which—

(*a*) falsely represents that the goods are of a particular standard, quality, quantity, grade, composition, style, or model

(*b*) falsely represents that the services are of a particular standard, quality, or grade

(*c*) falsely represents any re-built, second-hand, renovated, reconditioned, or old goods as new goods

(*d*) represents that the goods or services have sponsorship, approval, performance, characteristics, accessories, uses, or benefits that such goods or services do not have

(*e*) represents that the seller or the supplier has a sponsorship or approval or affiliation which such seller or supplier does not have

(*f*) makes a false or misleading representation concerning the need for, or the usefulness of, any goods or services

(*g*) gives to the public any warranty or guarantee of the performance, efficacy, or length of life of a product or of any goods that are not based on an adequate or proper test".[28]

Rights of the Consumer section 2(9)

The consumer rights are explained in the Sec.2(9) of *The Consumer Protection Act 2019*, this act's main focus is on spreading awareness of consumer rights to all consumers and making them comprehensible to the large sector of consumers, these rights are as follows:

"(*i*) the right to be protected against the marketing of goods, products, or services which are hazardous to life and property

(*ii*) the right to be informed about the quality, quantity, potency, purity, standard, and price of goods, products, or services, as the case may be, to protect the consumer against unfair trade practices

(*iii*) the right to be assured, wherever possible, access to a variety of goods, products or services at competitive prices

(*iv*) the right to be heard and to be assured that consumer's interests will receive due consideration at appropriate fora

(*v*) the right to seek redressal against unfair trade practices or restrictive trade practices or unscrupulous exploitation of consumers

(*vi*) the right to consumer awareness".[29]

Duties of the Consumer

The doctrine of *"Caveat Emptor"* means 'Let the buyer be aware' this doctrine places a burden on the buyer or consumer, to make a careful purchase, failure of which unable the buyer to recover the damages for the inconvenience faced by him from the seller.

When the seller sells the goods in the market, it is the duty of the buyer to examine the goods carefully and to make the proper selection of the goods before purchasing them blindly.

Government Initiatives for Consumer Awareness

"JaagoGrahakJaago" is a consumer awareness drive that was started in 2005 by the Ministry of consumers' affairs with an aim to educate and spread awareness. Targeted the consumer through multi-media platforms like through T.V, advertisements, social media, newspapers, etcspread awareness about various things related to consumer disputes, bank frauds, consumer authorities, food safety, etc. Making consumers aware of the provisions of The Consumer Protection Act and the rights and duties of the consumer.

Online initiatives such as:

- National consumer helpline mobile app.
- National consumer helpline shortcode 14404
- Barcode reader app.
- Online consumer communities
- Microsite for digitally safe consumer
- Online consumer mediation centre

➢ Guidelines issued by the Ministry of consumer affairs ensure the consumers about quality, purity, potency, standards, and price.

➢ Portal for Grievances Against Misleading Advertisements GAMA for protection of the consumers against misleading and deceptive advertisements.

➢ Setting up various national test housing agencies that conduct tests and evaluations of various products as per the set standards by the Ministry of consumer affairs.

➢ Quantity and Quality assurance to consumers through the Legal Metrology Act 2009 and Bureau of Indian Standard Act 1986 and the new BIS Act 2016.

➢ Price monitoring of the goods to save the consumers from unreasonable prices.

➢ Various consumer awareness programs in schools and colleges on the occasion of "National Consumer Day" and "World consumer rights day" on the topics like JagoGrahakJago, GrahakDost, UpbhoktaJagran, etc.

Consumer Protection Council Section 3-9

The consumer protection council was set up by the government of India at three levels Central, State, and District for the protection of consumer rights.

- *"Central Consumer Protection Council (section 3)-*It is established by the central government works as an advisory council and renders advice on the promotion and protection of consumers and their rights. Consisting of, a chairperson who is the minister-in-charge of the Department of consumer affairs at the central government and other members appointed by the central government".[30]

- *"State Consumer Protection Council (Section 6)-* It isestablished by the notification of the state government works as an advisory council and renders advice on the promotion and protection of consumers and their rights within the state. Consisting of the minister-in-charge of consumer affairs at the state government who act as a chairman other members appointed by the state government not exceeding ten".[31]

- ***"District Consumer Protection Council(Section 8)*-**It is established by the notification of the state government works as an advisory council and renders advice on the promotion and protection of consumers and their rights within the district. Consisting of a chairman, who is the district collector, and other members appointed by the state government".[32]

Central Consumer Protection Authority Section 10

The Central Consumer Protection Authority was established by the Central Government to regulate matters relating to the violation of the rights of consumers, unfair trade practices, and false or misleading advertisements which are prejudicial to the interests of the consumers and to promote, protect and enforce the rights of consumers as a class.

The Central Authority shall consist of a Chief Commissioner and other members as appointed by the Central Government. The headquarters of the Central Authority is situated in the National Capital Region Delhi and on the decision of the central government may have regional and other offices in other places in India. The Chief Commissioner has the powers of general superintendence, direction, and control in respect of all administrative matters of the Central Authority.

The Central Consumer Protection Authority holds the power to:

- Protect, promote, and enforce the rights of consumers and prevent violation of consumer rights.
- Prevent unfair trade practices and ensures that no person is engaged in such practices.
- Ensure that no false or misleading advertisements of any goods and services are published and which contravene the provisions of the act.

Dispute Resolution under the Consumer Protection Act

Consumer disputes can be resolved either by mediation or by filing a suit in Consumer Dispute Redressal Commission at the National, State, and District levels.

Mediation is a newly introduced consumer dispute resolution approach under the consumer protection act. The District Commission at any stage of the dispute, if notices that there are the elements of settlement that are also acceptable to the parties, may direct the parties to give in writing their consent to have their dispute settled by mediation. District commission within five days of the receipt of the consent may refer the matter for mediation.[33]

The process of the mediation is mentioned in Chapter 5 of the Consumer Protection Act 2019 under Sec. 74 to Sec. 81

Establishment of the Mediation Cell

The state government shall establish the Consumer Mediation Cell attached to the District Commission and State Commission of that state and the Central Government shall establish Consumer Mediation Cell attached to the National Commission.[34]

The commission may as per the case shall prepare a panel of mediators on the recommendation of a selection committee consisting of the President and a member of that commission.Mediation proceedings take place at the respective mediation cell and the mediator has to conduct the mediation in a time-bound manner. The mediator has to resolve the matter in a voluntary way which is accepted by both of the parties. If the mediation between the parties reaches a mutual agreement concerning all the issues involved in the dispute the parties shall sign the agreement and the mediator shall forward a settlement report to the concerned commission.Where there is no agreement reached and the settlement is not possible, the mediator shall prepare his report and forward the same to the concerned commission.

Consumer Disputes Redressal Commission

- *District Consumer Dispute Redressal Commission (section 28)-* if the mediation reaches no settlement the aggrieved party can move to District Dispute Redressal Commission.The state government shall establish a District Dispute Redressal Commissionin each district, consisting of a president and not less than two members prescribed or appointed by the state government.

  The jurisdiction of the District Commission is to entertain complaints below 50 lakhs and the local jurisdiction of the parties according to their residency or the place of trade. The suit can be filed within two years of the issue. A person can appeal to the state commission within 30 days after the decision of the District Commission is passed.

- *State Consumer Dispute Redressal Commission (Section 42)* -the state government shall establish a State Dispute Redressal Commission[35], consisting of a president and four other members including one woman compulsorily. Functioning at the state capital region and looking into matters of more than 50 lakhs and less than 2 crores. Hears the complaints against unfair trade practices and appeals against the orders of the district commission. The appeal to National Commission can be made within 30 days of the decision made by the State Commission.

- ***National Consumer Dispute Redressal Commission (Section 53)*** - the central government shall establish the National Consumer Dispute Redressal Commission[36], consisting of a president and four other members including one woman compulsorily. Functions at the National Capital Region and look into matters above 2 crores.Hears the issues regarding unfair practices and contracts, and appeals against state commission and the central authority. Calls for the record and passes the orders for the pending cases. Appeal to the Supreme Court can be made within thirty days.

Mediums to Spread Consumer Awareness

The Government has also launched various programs to spread consumer awareness but the only problem is, a large part of consumers are still unaware of their rights and duties and this becomes a hefty task.As a common man, I think of some ideas that can be taken into consideration for consumer awareness.

1. The banners of 6 consumer rights on every shop in India so that the visiting consumers can notice them in one sight.
2. The district collector may conduct some drills, and school programs, and also with the help of local drama clubs or students may conduct nukkadnataks or dramas at marketplaces
3. The topic Of Consumer Awareness and Empowerment should be made a compulsory part of a curriculum so that the young generation which is the young consumer sector can be made aware of their rights and duties
4. Make a small compulsory column in the newspaper about Consumer affairs and must educate the consumer according to daily ongoing consumer affairs and their rights, remedies, and other necessary pieces of information.
5. Some printed pamphlets with consumer rights and other necessary information mentioned on it should be distributed in each house which can be done by volunteers as an activity.
6. Wall paintings about consumer awareness in crowded marketplaces, and small books in comic way to teach consumer awareness can also be distributed.

Conclusion

Consumers are an essential part of the economy as we have already discussed in this chapter but to improve and make the consumer sector more aware and educated is today's task. The law is there the provisions are there the education about consumers is there but the only thing which is lacking is the reach to the consumers, despite all the initiatives taken by the government the reach to the consumers is required the large part of the consumer sector is unaware of their rights that becomes a problem for the nations. But slowly by following various measures and considering the evolving factor may overcome this lack of reach.

"Aware today, empowered tomorrow" In this chapter we have talked about consumer awareness and empowerment which is today's essential need, and mentioned all the rights, duties, various consumer protection authorities, consumer dispute redressal commissions, etc. to make the consumer smart which will make the future of economy bright. In the end, I will say "Awareness ignites change, and empowerment is the flame".

---

[1] Student of Maharishi University of Information technology, Maharishi Law School, BBA LLB (2nd year)

[2] Student of Maharishi University of Information technology, Maharishi Law School, BA LLB (2nd year)

[3] Student of Maharishi University of Information technology, Maharishi Law School, LLB (1 year)

[4] AIR 2009 SC 84

[5] AIR 2010 SC 235

[6] AIR2022SC4917

[7] Navtej Singh Johar and Ors. vs. Union of India (UOI) and Ors, AIR2018SC4321

[8] AIR2009SC84

[9] Manji Yamada *v.* Union of India & Ors, AIR2009SC84

[10] Supriyo v/s Union of India, WP (civil) 1011/2022

[11] AIR 2017 SC 4161

[12] AIR 2009 SC 84

[13] Manji Yamada *v.* Union of India & Ors, AIR2009SC84

[14] AIR2009SC84

[15] Manji Yamada *v.* Union of India & Ors AIR2009SC84

[16] Arun Muthuvel v. Union of India, W.P. (Civil) No. 756/2022

[17] https://www.livelaw.in/top-stories/surrogate-mother-need-not-be-genetically-related-to-child-centre-clarifies-surrogacy-law-provision-before-supreme-court-220977?infinitescroll=1

[18] W.P. (Civil) No. 756/2022

[19] A.I.R. 2002 S.C. 2931.

[20]Consumer Protection Act 2019,s.1.

[21]*Ibid,* s.2(7).

[22]*Ibid,* s.2(10).

[23]*Ibid,* s.2(11).

[24]*Ibid,* s.2(21).

[25]*Ibid,* s.2(41).

[26]*Ibid,* s.2(34).

[27]*Ibid,* s.2(41).

[28]*Ibid,* s.2(47).

[29]*Ibid,* s.2(9).

[30]*Ibid,* s.3.

[31]*Ibid,* s.6.

[32]*Ibid,* s.8.

[33] Consumer Protection Act ,2019,s.37.

[34] Consumer Protection Act, 2019,s.74.

[35]*Ibid,* s. 42.

[36]*Ibid,* s. 53.

THE END